COMPREHENSIVE RESEARCH
AND STUDY GUIDE

BLOOM'S
MAJOR
SHORT
STORY
W R I T E R S

John
Steinbeck

EDITED AND WITH AN
INTRODUCTION BY HAROLD BLOOM

BLOOM'S MAJOR SHORT STORY WRITERS

William Faulkner

F. Scott Fitzgerald

Ernest Hemingway

O. Henry

James Joyce

Herman Melville

Flannery O'Connor

Edgar Allan Poe

J. D. Salinger

John Steinbeck

Mark Twain

Eudora Welty

BLOOM'S MAJOR WORLD POETS

Geoffrey Chaucer

Emily Dickinson

John Donne

T. S. Eliot

Robert Frost

Langston Hughes

John Milton

Edgar Allan Poe

Shakespeare's Poems & Sonnets

Alfred, Lord Tennyson

Walt Whitman

William Wordsworth

COMPREHENSIVE RESEARCH
AND STUDY GUIDE

BLOOM'S
MAJOR
SHORT
STORY
WRITERS

John
Steinbeck

BLOOM

Introduction © 1999 by Harold Bloom

Printed and bound in the United States of America.

First Printing
1 3 5 7 9 8 6 4 2

ISBN: 0-7910-5125-0

Library of Congress Cataloging-in-Publication Data

John Steinbeck / edited and with an introduction by Harold Bloom.
p.   cm. — (Bloom's major short story writers)
Includes bibliographical references and index.
ISBN 0-7910-5125-0
1. Steinbeck, John, 1902-1968—Criticism and interpretation.
1. Short story.   I. Bloom, Harold.   II. Series.
PS3537.T3234Z7154   1998
813'52—dc21
98-49209
CIP

Chelsea House Publishers
1974 Sproul Road, Suite 400
Broomall, PA 19008-0914

Contributing Editor: Jennifer Lewin

Contents

User's Guide

This volume is designed to present biographical, critical, and bibliographical information on the author's best-known or most important short stories. Following Harold Bloom's editor's note and introduction is a detailed biography of the author, discussing major life events and important literary accomplishments. A plot summary of each short story follows, tracing significant themes, patterns, and motifs in the work, and an annotated list of characters supplies brief information on the main characters in each story.

A selection of critical extracts, derived from previously published material from leading critics, analyzes aspects of each short story. The extracts consist of statements from the author, if available, early reviews of the work, and later evaluations up to the present. A bibliography of the author's writings (including a complete list of all books written, cowritten, edited, and translated), a list of additional books and articles on the author and the work, and an index of themes and ideas in the author's writings conclude the volume.

～

Harold Bloom is Sterling Professor of the Humanities at Yale University and Henry W. and Albert A. Berg Professor of English at the New York University Graduate School. He is the author of over 20 books and the editor of more than 30 anthologies of literary criticism.

Professor Bloom's works include *Shelley's Mythmaking* (1959), *The Visionary Company* (1961), *Blake's Apocalypse* (1963), *Yeats* (1970), *A Map of Misreading* (1975), *Kabbalah and Criticism* (1975), and *Agon: Toward a Theory of Revisionism* (1982). *The Anxiety of Influence* (1973) sets forth Professor Bloom's provocative theory of the literary relationships between the great writers and their predecessors. His most recent books include *The American Religion* (1992), *The Western Canon* (1994), *Omens of Millennium: The Gnosis of Angels, Dreams, and Resurrection* (1996), and *Shakespeare: The Invention of the Human* (1998).

Professor Bloom earned his Ph.D. from Yale University in 1955 and has served on the Yale faculty since then. He is a 1985 MacArthur Foundation Award recipient and served as the Charles Eliot Norton Professor of Poetry at Harvard University in 1987–88. He is currently the editor of other Chelsea House series in literary criticism, including BLOOM'S NOTES, BLOOM'S MAJOR POETS, MAJOR LITERARY CHARACTERS, MODERN CRITICAL VIEWS, MODERN CRITICAL INTERPRETATIONS, and WOMEN WRITERS OF ENGLISH AND THEIR WORKS.

Editor's Note

My Introduction meditates upon the limits of Steinbeck's art in his story, "The Chrysanthemums."

As there are a copious number of critical views extracted, I will comment only upon a few high points. David Leon Higdon shrewdly notes that "The Chrysanthemums" presents Elisa in imagery that suggests a Maenad or Bacchic initiate, while the poet-novelist Jay Parini comments upon the role of gardening in the story.

"The White Quail," another story in which Steinbeck reflects the influence of D. H. Lawrence, is seen by Marilyn Mitchell as a parable of failed perfectionism, after which John H. Timmerman argues that Mary Teller's stance in the story represents a belated High Romanticism.

"Flight" is judged by Peter Lisca not to resolve its contradictory impulses. Mimi Gladstein emphasizes the role of Mama Torres as one of Steinbeck's women who can endure despite all pressures.

The stories of *The Red Pony* are probably Steinbeck's most famous but they have palpable flaws, as well as considerable emotional force. The critical views available on *The Red Pony* are useful in analyzing that force, as will be seen in this volume. Readers of *The Red Pony*, still a popular book, never can be quite certain whether they are encountering disillusionment or sentimentality, an ambiguity that is generic in Steinbeck.

Introduction

HAROLD BLOOM

Eudora Welty, writing about the short stories of D. H. Lawrence, memorably caught the essential strangeness of Lawrence's art of representation.

> For the truth seems to be that Lawrence's characters don't really speak their words—not conversationally, not to one another—they are *not* speaking on the street, but are playing like fountains or radiating like the moon or storming like the sea, or their silence is the silence of wicked rocks. It is borne home to us that Lawrence is writing of our human relationships on earth in terms of eternity, and these terms set Lawrence's form. The author himself appears in authorship in places like the moon, and sometimes smiles on us while we stand there under him.

Welty was a short story writer almost of Lawrence's eminence; John Steinbeck was not. But Steinbeck's stories owed as much to Lawrence as Steinbeck's novels did to Hemingway. Though he resented Hemingway, Steinbeck wrote a softened version of Hemingway's famous style. Lawrence affected Steinbeck very differently; something in Steinbeck implicitly understood that his own naturalistic reductionism limited his art. D. H. Lawrence's heroic vitalism, his ability to endow his character with qualities "playing like fountains," appealed to Steinbeck's repressed transcendentalism. The best of Steinbeck's stories are in Lawrence's mode, and not Hemingway's.

"The Chrysanthemums," which seems to me the most interesting of Steinbeck's stories, is far closer to Lawrence's intense evocations of the soul than it is to the version of Darwinism that Steinbeck had taken over from the marine biologist Edward Ricketts. Several critics have noted how close Steinbeck's Elisa Allen is to Lawrence's March in *The Fox,* except that Elisa is a balked figure from the beginning. Her repressed sexuality, aroused by the encounter with the wandering tinker, is not likely to be gratified by her inadequate husband, or indeed by any other man. In Lawrence, Elisa would become a lover of women, but Steinbeck evades such an intimation, though the imaginative logic of his story probably argues for such a future.

How much change takes place in Elisa between the start and the conclusion of the story? When we first see her, she is all potential, a force not yet exercised although she is in the middle of the journey.

> She was cutting down the old year's chrysanthemum stalks with a pair of short and powerful scissors. She looked down toward the men by the tractor shed now and then. Her face was eager and mature and handsome; even her work with the scissors was over-eager, over-powerful. The chrysanthemum stems seemed too small and easy for her energy.

At the story's close, she is crying weakly, "as if she were an old woman." We need to know more if we are to understand whether this is only a momentary defeat or the reassertion of a pattern. In Lawrence or in Welty we *would* know, because both of them were able to write "of our human relationships on earth in terms of eternity." Steinbeck as a writer never could achieve that, not even in *The Grapes of Wrath*. "The Chrysanthemums" shows Steinbeck bruising himself against his own imaginative limitations, unable to bruise himself an exit from himself. The materia poetica for a larger and more intense art is there in the story, but Steinbeck could not realize it. ❀

Biography of
John Steinbeck

(1902–1968)

John Ernst Steinbeck was born in Salinas, California, to Olive Hamilton Steinbeck and John Ernst Steinbeck on February 27, 1902. As a young boy he summered by the Pacific Ocean near Monterey. During this time he acquired his own pony, Jill, his father taught him to garden, and he read widely in the classics—especially loving the works of Sir Thomas Malory. He performed well enough in school to skip the fifth grade. In 1918, he became ill with pneumonia and almost died, but he recovered. The following year he graduated from Salinas High School and attended Stanford University, majoring in English; his attendance was sporadic until 1925, when he left without a degree. His university experience led to his start as a writer, however; the *Stanford Spectator* published some of his satire in June 1925. After leaving Stanford, Steinbeck worked as a manual laborer while continuing to write.

In 1927, his story "The Gifts of Iban" was published in *The Smoker's Companion* under the pseudonym John Stern. Deciding it would be too difficult to work in a warehouse and write at the same time, he moved into his parents' summer cottage in Pacific Grove. Their financial support enabled him to focus on writing. In 1929, good news came in the form of Robert McBride's $2,250 advance for the publication of *Cup of Gold*, his first novel. Later that year he moved to San Francisco to work on his next book *To a God Unknown;* he also read Hemingway for the first time. His relationship with Carol Henning, whom he met while working at a hatchery in Tahoe, began to inspire in him a deep social conscience. Her interest in the plight of the poor influenced his moral stance in *Of Mice and Men* and *The Grapes of Wrath.* They secretly married in 1930, settling in a suburb of Los Angeles. Steinbeck began to be discouraged by the poor reception of his works and his financial dependence on his and Carol's parents (who were feeling the impact of the Depression), so in 1931 he moved back to the family cottage to work on a collection of stories, *The Pastures of Heaven.* A crucial intellectual friendship with Edward F. Ricketts, a marine biologist and ecologist with a laboratory on Cannery Row, also formed during this time. The two men found in each other a similar approach to life and Steinbeck admired the technical side of Ricketts' laboratory work and his effusive, bold personality. *Sea of Cortez* (1941) is based on their 1940 journey to the Gulf of California. Ricketts died in 1948, and Steinbeck published a memoir entitled "About Ed Ricketts."

The Pastures of Heaven was accepted by Cape and Smith in 1932, and in 1933 his next novel, *To a God Unknown*, appeared. None of these early literary efforts attracted critical attention. His financial situation was dire, he was in despair about the state of his vocation, and his mother was dying. But things began to pick up when he began to publish many of the stories that would appear in the 1938 collection *The Long Valley*, as well as the novel *Tortilla Flat* in 1935. The high point of his career to that point, *Tortilla Flat* tells of a Monterey paisano, Danny, his dissolute friends, and their collective resemblance to King Arthur's Round Table. It got good reviews and was named Best Novel of 1935 by the Commonwealth Club of California.

In Dubious Battle (1936), however, was more indicative of the kind of saga that was to preoccupy Steinbeck for most of his career. It tells of Jim Nolan, a labor organizer, and the strike he organizes among migrant apple pickers. After writing it, he then toured California's Central Valley where Eric Thomsen of the Resettlement Administration showed him the radical difference in the quality of life between migrants with and without government aid. Steinbeck was shocked at what he saw and wrote news articles on the conditions. When the situation worsened because of flooding, Steinbeck wrote a story for *Life* which was rejected for its bitter truthfulness. His conscience could not allow him to do nothing for the children who were dying of starvation and illness.

Meanwhile, his literary reputation was growing. *Of Mice and Men* (1937) was a Book-of-the-Month Club selection and sold 117,000 copies. The reviews were positive, and it launched his popular recognition. The novella—still considered his most popular short work, along with *The Pearl* and *The Red Pony*—concerns two bindle stiffs, mentor George Milton and mentally challenged Lennie, who want to own their own farm. In it Steinbeck tries to retain an "objective" stance, reporting the story as "something that happened" rather than giving a justification for it. John and Carol celebrated its success by going to Europe via New York where they spent two weeks with "high society" (shy, modest John would never become comfortable with the New York literary set). On their way home they stopped in Washington, D.C. to discuss his idea for a novel about the Dust Bowl workers with the Farm Security Administration. After he returned home, the play version of *Of Mice and Men* opened in New York, where it met with great success. After this, Steinbeck would turn many of his texts into film and play scripts, a practice that would sometimes work well, and sometimes fail.

Steinbeck worked on a novel about migrant workers, which was to become *The Grapes of Wrath*, in 1938, while his agents assembled the collection *The Long Valley* from many stories he had published in the early to mid-1930s. It is named after the long, narrow, arable strip of land around Salinas. Many of the other stories in the collection, like "The Chrysanthemums," "The White Quail," "The Murder," and "The Snake" are stories of domestic life in which estranged, dreadfully unhappy couples or individuals have great difficulty establishing meaningful human relationships. The reviews of *The Long Valley* ranged from tepid to enthusiastic; readers liked the series *The Red Pony* best of all, and did not know how to react to the tales of difficult marriages.

In 1939, *The Grapes of Wrath*, Steinbeck's most famous novel, was published amidst harsh government speculations that Steinbeck was a communist sympathizer, allegations which would prove particularly troubling in the McCarthy era. The novel's subject is the sharecropping Joad family, who travel along the well-worn Route 66 from Oklahoma to California in search of the American Dream. The novel did much to identify Steinbeck's social preoccupations with the plight of the poor migrants and especially with the relationship between the people living on the land and the landscape itself. It won the Pulitzer Prize in 1940, and the highly successful movie version, directed by John Ford, was filmed on location with the advice of Steinbeck's friend Tom Collins.

In 1941, he wrote an anti-German propaganda piece, *The Moon is Down,* and worked for the Foreign Information Service. The novel sold well; however, Steinbeck's marriage was deteriorating, and he deluded himself into thinking that he and his wife could continue.

He finally divorced Carol in 1943 after having started an affair with the young Gwyndolen Conger. He married Gwyn the same year. At about the same time, and with the help of Eleanor Roosevelt, he got the New York ban on *The Forgotten Village* (deemed too "socialist") lifted. He lived in New York City with Gwyn until 1943 when he returned to California to start the film script of Bombs Away, a work extolling the virtues of the Air Force. He also wrote the film script for Alfred Hitchcock's *Lifeboat*. He was briefly sent to Europe to write dispatches that were later collected in *Once There Was a War* (1958), and he traveled to England, Italy, and North Africa. When he returned to Manhattan life with Gwyn, he published *Cannery Row,* the story of that section of Monterey where Ricketts' lab flourished amidst sardine canneries, brothels, and dilapidated housing.

In 1947, *The Pearl* sold 750,000 copies but garnered little critical notice. His second marriage was falling apart in the late forties, and he left with the photographer Robert Capa for Moscow to create a photoessay on Russian life. Gwyn went with them as far as Paris, leaving their two sons at home. *A Russian Journal* was published in 1948, the same year that the film version of *The Pearl* was released. Steinbeck was elected to the American Academy of Arts and Letters in the early fifties, and he began work on *East of Eden* (1952). During this period, he divorced Gwyn and moved into the Bedford Hotel. In 1949, the film version of *The Red Pony* appeared. Also, he met Elaine Scott, wife of actor Zachary Scott, whom he married the next year after her divorce. This third marriage turned out to be his happiest and final one. In 1951, he settled in New York City with Elaine, and they begin summering in Nantucket.

The last fifteen years of his life were filled with a fairly steady routine: once a year Steinbeck wrote and released a major book or a screenplay, then spent time in Europe with Elaine. This period produced *Viva Zapata!, East of Eden, Pipe Dream, Sweet Thursday,* and *The Short Reign of Pippin IV.* While in Paris, Steinbeck wrote literary articles for *Le Figaro.* He defended his friend and playwright Arthur Miller before the House Un-American Activities committee in 1957. In his last ten years Steinbeck spent much time recuperating from illness on Capri and vacationing in England, a country with which he felt a great affinity from boyhood because of his obsession with Malory's tales of the Round Table. He also became a favorite author for the United States Government's cultural missions to Eastern

Europe and the Soviet Union. Steinbeck was a popular novelist in those countries and visited them frequently.

His last bestseller, published in 1962, was *Travels with Charley*, in which he recounted his journey across America with his dog in a converted pickup truck. "Unlike any other Steinbeck," wrote the *New York Herald Tribune*; "One of the best books John Steinbeck has ever written," stated the *Boston Herald*. He was awarded the Nobel Prize in literature the same year.

His support of the Vietnam War in his final years came as a shock to some. He toured Asia in 1967, discussing his trip with President Johnson and Secretary of Defense Robert McNamara. In 1968 he suffered several heart attacks while summering in Sag Harbor. He died in New York City on December 20, and his ashes were taken by Elaine to Pacific Grove and then buried in the family plot in Salinas. ❀

Plot Summaries of
The Red Pony Stories

The four stories that comprise *The Red Pony* were published separately and sequentially in the 1930s (with the exception of "The Leader of the People," which was published in London in 1936, a year before "The Promise" appeared in the United States). They appeared together for the first time in *The Long Valley* (1938), and in a separate volume titled *The Red Pony* in 1945. The stories trace the early years of Jody Tiflin, a young boy living in the Salinas valley of California.

The Gift

In the first story, Jody is 10 years old, obedient, quiet, and bashful. The school year has just begun. He is a shrewd observer of farm life, able to detect the type of shoes his father is wearing, for example, by the sound of his steps in the kitchen. He silently yearns to join his father, Carl, and their hired hand, Billy Buck, on their errands into town, but instead he dutifully goes on his way, greeting the family dogs and chickens, drinking from a spring, and presenting himself for his mother's inspection before school starts. On the day of the story he senses change in the air. His foibles are innocent and typical of young boys: he squashes a green muskmelon under his foot and, easily embarrassed by his peccadillo, hides it; then he goes off to school.

When he returns, his mother chides him for having barely done his chores the day before, and after finishing them on this day he takes out his rifle and aims it at things. He will have to wait two years until he receives a cartridge, but his father, a disciplinarian, wanted to give him the gun to try his patience.

The following day, Carl and Billy take Jody out to the barn to see the red pony colt they have acquired for him at a sheriff's auction in town. Jody is shocked and delighted at having been given his very own pony, a boy's dream, and all the new responsibilities of caring for it are like a badge of honor. He names the pony Gabilan after "the grandest and prettiest thing he knew," the western mountains. Billy warns him of the patience he'll need to train the pony, since having come from a show, Gabilan is a long way from being fit for riding. Jody will need to break him in, and he is eager to assume that daunting task.

Among his peers, Jody quickly earns admiration and authority as a young horseman in training. Under Billy's direction, he grooms Gabilan and faithfully attends to his needs with love and affection. The pony becomes an all-consuming passion, with Jody spending most of his free time with him during waking hours, but being possessed at night by horrific visions of the pony's illness and other potential dangers.

A crucial component of the boy-pony relationship is Gabilan's tendency to misbehave. Jody is alternately thrilled and frightened by him, and when the pony's rapid growth means that Jody can begin to ride him by Thanksgiving, he prepares with both excitement and trepidation. He is afraid of falling off the horse—not only for the conventional reason of not wanting to shame himself and disappoint Carl and Billy, but also because, secretly, he fears Gabilan's violent reaction.

Rain at Thanksgiving means that Jody cannot yet begin riding. Also, the foul weather necessitates Jody's vigilance in keeping Gabilan inside, away from the danger of catching cold. One day Billy Buck promises to take Gabilan inside if it rains while Jody is at school, but he forgets, and Jody returns home to a cold and shivering pony. Billy feels guilty and does everything in his power to help Jody nurse him back to health, but nothing works. The pony's condition rapidly worsens and Jody becomes disillusioned by both Billy's failure and his persistent optimism in the face of the pony's bad health. Jody must simultaneously juggle his conflicting feelings of betrayal by Billy with his realization of human fallibility in general. Thus, the title "The Gift" acquires a bittersweet ring, since with the gift of the pony comes the unexpected gift of a lesson about human nature.

Carl has a difficult time relating to his son's misery. Instead of advice and support, he offers him jokes after dinner one night, much to Jody and Billy's disappointment. When a lump in Gablian's throat swells, Billy offers to cut it to make a breathing hole. Jody stays, as always, by his pony's side, despite the agonizing pain of watching him suffer. Steinbeck's harrowing descriptions of Gabilan's reactions to the blade at his throat are painfully real. The pony refuses to eat and Jody knows that its end is approaching. He spends the pony's last night in his company, awakening at every difficult breath. In the morning Gabilan has disappeared, and Jody follows his tracks to find him laying in a clearing while buzzards swarm around him waiting for the moment to dive in for their carrion. In anger and frustration at Gabilan's death, he cruelly kills one of the birds. His father chides him, but Billy, who has the story's last word, is sympathetic to his situation.

The Great Mountains
Our first glimpse of Jody in this story reveals a slightly more violent, deviously playful boy than the innocent youth of "The Gift." He sets traps for the dog, throws rocks at him, and kills and disembowels a bird, but still feels ashamed, as he had with the green muskmelon, at the possibility of discovery. A different aspect of his personality, but one which equally shows his desire for excitement, is his curiosity about the western Coast Range, the great mountains. He receives no satisfactory answer as to what is on or over them from either parent or from Billy Buck. Still intrigued by the mountains, he sees a man approaching the house from the Salinas road. He looks old, weary, properly dressed and respectable, bony, and ageless. He introduces himself as Gitano and claims to have returned to the former site of his family ranch. Jody finds him mysterious and fascinating, his mother is uncertain, Billy is understanding, and Carl acts in an openly cruel and hostile manner, saying he cannot afford the expense of caring for a dying man on his farm. Carl allows Gitano to stay the night, however, and when Jody shows him to his room, he eagerly asks if Gitano has been to the great mountains. Gitano's thoughtful reply in the affirmative, that the mountains had been "nice" and "quiet," fuels Jody's desire to experience them for himself and quickly inspires Jody's deep admiration.

Before dinner, Gitano sees Easter, their 30-year-old horse, and Carl talks of wanting to shoot him to put him out of the misery of old, useless age. Billy disagrees, and says he deserves a dignified life after long, productive years of work, taking Gitano's side in a debate that is ostensibly about the horse. The narrator, very much sympathetic to Jody's perspective, comments that Carl tries to hurt Gitano as he had tried to hurt Jody many times before. Jody tries to soften his father's words but feels their pain. At dinner, Mrs. Tiflin feels sorry for Gitano and wishes to keep him. Carl insists on sending Gitano off to his nearby family, and Gitano repeats his mantra: "I was born here." Jody hears this declaration as an intimation of Gitano's deep connection with the great mountains, old and sturdy and mysterious. After dinner, Jody visits Gitano and gets him to show his beautiful, golden rapier, a treasured gift from his father. It excites Jody to have been shown such a secret object.

In the morning, Gitano rises before everybody else and disappears with Easter. He was spotted by a neighbor, and Carl decides to leave the two of them alone. Jody thinks he sees them in the distance near the great mountains, and, filled with "a nameless sorrow," wishes he could cry to assuage his "longing." His compassion for Gitano, the old *paisano*, enables him to feel a stronger bond than his elders with the land and its history. His vision of the rapier makes Gitano even more heroic and chivalric, like a modern King Arthur of the Round Table.

The Promise

As the story begins, Carl Tiflin asks Jody if he would like a new pony of his own, under the condition that he works for the five dollars it will cost them to mate their mare Nellie with neighbor Jess Taylor's stallion. Thrilled, Jody agrees to take on the necessary work and to bring Nellie to the Taylor ranch for the mating. He feels more like a man and works harder at his tasks than ever before. When Jody accompanies Nellie on the appointed day, he is frightened by the violent behavior that characterizes horses mating. He thinks that Nellie will be killed when he sees the stallion race towards her and attack her. For the rest of the spring and summer Jody works extra hard for his father, learning additional chores such as how to milk a cow. He cares for Nellie because she will be the mother of his pony. It is evident to him, however, that she is Billy Buck's favorite horse, and out of affection for boy and horse Billy provides Jody with an education about her pregnancy and what kinds of expectations he should have. Because he had been negligent before, when Gabilan became ill from being in the rain, Billy is careful not to misrepresent Nellie's chances of having a strong colt, but at the same time he is excited for Jody. He makes it clear, for example, that sometimes the colt is in the wrong position when the mare is ready to deliver, and the colt must be killed in order for the mare to survive. This time, Billy knows better than to promise that Jody will have his colt, and while he does not like being negative before the optimistic and enthusiastic boy, he is compelled not to mislead him in any way. He is also filled with the painful feeling that Jody mistrusts him because of what happened to the pony Gabilan.

Jody fantasizes about having a stallion, cruel to all but him, named Black Demon. He wants to perform good deeds and win contests with Demon. In his ego-building daydream, Jody imagines he and the horse winning over all other rodeo contestants in steer roping. His final fantasy has him being called on by the president of the United States to capture a bandit.

When autumn comes, his mother teaches him how to feed Nellie to keep her healthy, and Billy continues to nurse Nellie and prepare her for giving birth. Billy's caring indicates the deep level of feeling he has for the mare. After a wait that seems like forever to the boy— Steinbeck is masterful at describing the boy's anticipation and impatience—Nellie is ready to throw the colt in mid-January. On the morning of delivery, Billy feels her womb and the colt seems to be positioned badly, so he becomes anxious and asks Jody to leave in order to shield him from the violent act he will have to commit. Jody refuses to leave, even while Billy is cursing at him, forcing Billy to perform a gruesome task in front of him. Billy kills Nellie with several hammer blows to the forehead. He pulls the colt out of her stomach, severs the umbilical cord, and while completely covered in blood and entrails he plants the colt at Jody's feet, just as he had promised.

Dumbfounded, Jody cannot move. Billy's deeply ambivalent expression can be read as evidence of horror at his own capacity to act in a way that upholds his promise to Jody, no matter what the cost. Being so close to Nellie, the cost of the mare's life is difficult for him to bear, but his own pride and conscience forced him to make the most difficult choice. At the story's powerful ending, Jody finds it difficult to celebrate the colt's birth, given that "the haunted, tired eyes of Billy Buck hung in the air ahead of him." Both Jody and Billy seem to have grown infinitely older because of the experience.

The Leader of the People
This final story in the collection offers a sympathetic recounting of a visit to the Tiflin ranch by Jody's maternal grandfather. The letter that has arrived later than it should have reveals that Mrs. Tiflin's father is on his way. Jody's father, Carl, bitterly complains at this prospect because all Grandfather ever seems to do, according to him, is talk about "the good old days" when men were men and "westering," or heading for the California coast. Grandfather bragged he

led a wagon train west; he was so proud of this singular accomplishment that he hardly talked about anything else. Mrs. Tiflin is much more sympathetic with her father's stories, because she recognizes how important they are to him, despite their countless reiteration and lack of variety.

On the morning of his grandfather's arrival, Jody revels in the idea of bringing in the dogs to hunt the mice that might emerge from where a haystack has been removed. His father playfully calls him "Big-Britches" for his nosiness. When Grandfather appears, Jody runs down the hill to meet him, observing his dignified, careful, slow movements. Like Gitano of "The Great Mountains," Grandfather has a mysterious air about him. When he comes into the house, he is warmly greeted. When he sees Billy Buck, Grandfather reminisces, as he always does, about having known Buck's father, Mule-tail Buck. Billy has a soft spot for Grandfather and listens to his stories of how he nearly died from starvation while crossing the plains. Grandfather reminds the family countless times that he was "the leader" of the group and had to be responsible for them. Whenever he asks if he has already told a story, Carl can barely contain his impatience, and Grandfather seems upset. At last, Carl interrupts him, but Grandfather tells Jody that he will continue the story later.

Jody sympathizes with Grandfather; as he had with Gitano in "The Great Mountains," he tries to compensate for his father's meanness. Everything reminds Grandfather of his great adventure, and while Billy, Jody, and Mrs. Tiflin sit through his stories, Carl taunts him both to his face and behind it, and when he tells his wife "now it's finished" and Grandfather should put the past behind him, Grandfather overhears him. He is saddened, agrees with Carl, and says he will not tell any more stories unless people want to hear them. Jody cheerfully says he likes to hear them. Grandfather confesses feeling hurt and unwanted, and even begins to question the very purpose of his heroic crossing of the desert.

The most important moment of the tale comes towards the end, during his conversation with Jody, when he reveals that he does not want to tell the stories for themselves but for the reaction he solicits in people. The crucial image is of the entire group of westering folk as "one big crawling beast" that had a will of its own and needed a head. He happened to be the head. There had been somewhere to go, a purpose to his and the other pioneers' movements, and he filled the job as their leader. It is not his own merit he extols when retelling the stories, but rather just the fact of its having happened. In a lyrical, Biblical moment, he says, "Then we came down to the sea, and it was done." The American people had reached their western frontier and the task of living there was upon them.

Jody asks if he can carry on the work; Grandfather says no, that it is all completed. It is unclear at the end of the story whether or not Grandfather has had a realization that his life's work was not as monumental as he had imagined it being and whether that revelation hurts or comforts him. Grandfather's acknowledgment that his great task in life is finished could either signal his acceptance of death or the beginning of his quest to enjoy his remaining days. ❀

List of Characters in
The Red Pony Stories

Jody Tiflin: A young boy who ages from ten to twelve years old during the course of the stories, Jody lives on a ranch with his family in the Salinas Valley. He enjoys all the devious delights of boyhood, such as throwing stones at birds and dogs, as well as playing with lizards and filling his lunch pail with creatures. He especially yearns for a pony and on two occasions gets one: Gabilan is bought for him at a sheriff's auction ("The Gift") and Nellie throws a colt ("The Promise"). He is obedient and respectful of authority, though Billy Buck's negligence in the case of Gabilan's death provides him with a lesson in human fallibility.

Billy Buck: He is the hired hand on the Tiflin ranch. A close friend of Carl Tiflin, and Jody's mentor, Billy Buck does many manual chores around the ranch and is usually very responsible. He waits for Carl to come into the kitchen for meals before entering himself, a sign of his awareness of social hierarchy. He is sympathetic to the plights of Gitano ("The Great Mountains") and Grandfather ("The Leader of the People") in the face of Carl's hostility, and he has a special relationship with Jody, whose affection for animal life he fosters and appreciates.

Carl Tiflin: Jody's father, Carl is a stern disciplinarian. He tries to instill a strong sense of responsibility in Jody and will give him gifts, like his rifle, before he gives him the cartridges for it, just to teach him patience. He is obeyed by all on the farm, though occasional jokes are made in his absence about his unsuccessful farming ideas. At times he can be cruel, as when he taunts Gitano and Grandfather, and hurt by others' reactions to his own insensitivity.

Mrs. Tiflin: Jody's mother is a kind, hardworking homemaker who does not allow Jody to slack off in his chores and who also knows how to pamper him when he is hurting, such as when his pony dies. She typically does not approve of Carl and Billy's decision to take Jody away from his school activities in order to be with them, but reluctantly agrees to cooperate with their schemes. ❀

Critical Views on
The Red Pony Stories

[Peter Lisca has written *The Wide World of John Steinbeck* (1958) and *John Steinbeck: Nature and Myth* (1978). In the first excerpt Lisca discusses Steinbeck's aritculation of the "group-man" theory in "The Leader of the People":]

Through the garrulous grandfather Steinbeck poses the question of the meaning and place which the frontier spirit should have in our time. Through each character's attitude toward the grandfather, in whom the tradition is embodied, the author explores a distinct reaction to the American pioneer past. For Carl, it is something done with. The West Coast has been reached and now the job is one of consolidation. It is boring and pointless to dwell on the heroic deeds of our past: "Now it's finished. Nobody wants to hear about it over and over." In this dismissal there is perhaps an unconscious resentment of his own unheroic life. To Carl's wife, the daughter of Grandfather, the stories of the past are just as boring, but her attitude is more respectful. She listens out of loyalty, knowing what this past meant to her forebears. Billy Buck's attitude is a little more complicated. His own father was a mule packer under Grandfather's leadership, and he himself retains much of the self-reliant, able-handed spirit of the heroic past. He listens with respect born of understanding. For Jody, as for any other American youngster, this past was a time of excitement: Indians, wagon trains, scouts, crossing the plains.

Yet it is to Jody that the grandfather is finally able to communicate the double aspect of the meaning behind his tales of Indians and wagon trains: "It wasn't Indians that were important, nor adventures, nor even getting out here. It was a whole bunch of people made into one big crawling beast. And I was the head. It was westering and westering. Every man wanted something for himself, but the big beast that was all of them wanted only westering. I was the leader, but if I hadn't been there, someone else would have been the head. The thing had to have a head." This is an important statement for an understanding of Steinbeck's group-man concept. The analogy of men to a "big crawling beast" was not intended to put, and in the context of Steinbeck's work does not put, men on the same moral basis as animals. Rather, it points out the energy that is released when the many desires of men can find expression in one unifying activity or aspiration. As the old man continues, it becomes evident that although "westering" may bear a superficial resemblance to animal migration, the impetus which drove his people had its roots not in the flesh but in the human spirit: "No place to go, Jody. Every place is taken. But that's not the worst—no, not the worst. Westering has died out of people. Westering isn't a hunger any more. It's all done."

Grandfather's statement is supported not only by Carl Tiflin and his wife, but by a continuum of symbols firmly embedded in the story. The physical setting is alive not with Indians and buffaloes but with small and petty game—gophers, snakes, pigeons, crows, rabbits, squirrels, and mice. And these mice, which Jody sets out to kill early in the story, are, significantly, still alive at its end, fat and comfortable in a rotting haystack. Yet, the story is not a sentimental glorification of a heroic past set against a mean and complacent present. The frontier *is* gone. Jody's excitement about killing the mice is not, as Grandfather sees it, a symbol of a degenerating race. Carl Tiflin and his wife are not cruel and stupid, but competent for the tasks at hand; their boredom with the old man's garrulousness is made understandable. Furthermore, in a very important sense it is Grandfather who has failed, in two ways. He has failed to adjust himself to the unavoidable fact that he could not go on being "the leader of the people" after the Pacific Ocean was reached. More important, despite his garrulousness he has failed to communicate to the new generation that "westering" was more than just killing Indians and eating buffalo meat.

Perhaps the ultimate wisdom in the story belongs to Billy Buck. When Jody remarks to him that the fat mice he intends to kill "don't know what's going to happen to them today," Billy Buck replies philosophically, "No, nor you either, nor me, nor anyone." Jody is "staggered" by this thought; he "knew it was true." This is Jody's lesson in history, the meaning of the past. Grandfather's frontier, like Frederick Jackson Turner's, was not so much a physical manifestation as an attitude of mind and a spirit which needs reviving in our time. Life is always a risk. The call for heroism is heard today as it was yesterday. The need for a leader of the people is still real, for we are all pioneers, forever crossing the dangerous and the unknown.

—Peter Lisca, *The Wide World of John Steinbeck* (New Brunswick, N.J.: Rutgers University Press, 1958): pp. 105–106.

[In this extract from *John Steinbeck: Nature and Myth*
(1978), Lisca discusses the tests that Jody undergoes in the
stories that are part of the *Red Pony* cycle:]

The initiation theme of these stories is clearly prepared for by Steinbeck's early stressing of Jody's childhood by various actions on his
part that denote a lack of adult status: his not being allowed to shoot
his rifle, the way he does his chores, etc. Yet, at the same time Jody
feels "an uncertainty in the air, a feeling of change and of loss and of
the gain of new and unfamiliar things." Steinbeck was well versed in
Frazer's *The Golden Bough,* which contains a chapter on puberty
rites, the ceremonies used by various cultures to mark the transition
from childhood to adulthood. These ceremonies generally have certain elements in common. They begin with a separation of the boy
from his mother and the world of childhood; this is often symbolized by a ritual death. There follows some ordeal to test the candi-
date's courage, after which he is for a period instructed in the sacred
lore of his tribe. He then experiences a symbolic rebirth into the
adult world. Although Steinbeck incorporated some version of all
these elements, naturally they are not all part of one experience as
they would be in a primitive culture. Rather, these elements are scattered over a period of time, as they are in other stories of initiation—Faulkner's "The Bear," Crane's *The Red Badge of Courage,*
Hemingway's Nick Adams stories, etc.

Frequently, tribal initiations begin unexpectedly and with no indi-
cation of their purpose. Thus Jody is sent to bed one evening under
circumstances which arouse his curiosity, for he feels his father has
important news of some kind. But he is told, "Never you mind. You
better get to bed." The following morning his father "crossly" com-
mands him to accompany himself and Billy Buck to an unstated
place for an unstated purpose. Jody "had trouble with his food then,
for he felt a kind of doom in the air." His mother expresses concern
that the men may keep him from school (childhood). That the men
had just returned from taking cattle to be slaughtered perhaps adds
to Jody's apprehension, for he is very sensitive to life and death symbols: the mossy spring and the cypress tree where hogs are
butchered, which they pass on this significant morning. As an American Indian's ordeal might be to survive a period alone in the wilderness and bring back an eagle feather, Jody's task turns out to be that

he must care for the red pony, which his father threatens to sell if Jody fails in any way, and during this period Jody "tortures himself" with fears of failing. The climax of this ordeal is to be the breaking of the pony "around Thanksgiving." Jody is very concerned that he not fail this test, and thinks of all the wrong things he could do, such as using his hands to stay on the bucking pony by grabbing the saddle horn: "Perhaps his father and Billy Buck would never speak to him again, they would be so ashamed." He also fears what the other boys will think if he does poorly: "it was too awful to think about." In a tribal community, failing the test could have such serious consequences as complete social ostracism. That this test never materializes and Jody is presented instead with a new and unexpected ordeal, the pony's sickness and death, is also a parallel to the pattern of initiation rites, in which boys are often deliberately misled as to the real nature of their ordeal.

In many cultures, the ordeal consists in some part of some significant wound, usually circumcision. This Steinbeck accomplishes symbolically through the red pony with which Jody has become identified. (Frazer cites examples of such totem animals.) The description of the tracheotomy that Billy Buck performs on the pony is strikingly similar to that of a circumcision, and Jody feels all the terror and anxiety he would feel for himself. The death of the red pony, the totem animal, signifies the death of Jody as a boy. His courageous but "ignorant" fight with the buzzard which has started to eat his pony is the story's final learning experience, in which he becomes aware of the existence of death and evil in the world view which is his inheritance as an adult. As in many initiation rites, his face is daubed with blood.

—Peter Lisca, *John Steinbeck: Nature and Myth* (Toronto: Fitzhenry & Whiteside Ltd., 1978): pp. 196–98.

WARREN FRENCH ON JODY'S MORAL GROWTH IN "THE GREAT MOUNTAINS"

[Warren French is professor of English at Indiana University-Purdue University, Indianapolis, Indiana. Among his numerous publications are *John Steinbeck* (1961; rev. 1975), *J. D. Salinger* (1963; rev. 1976), and *The Social Novel at the End of an Era* (1966). The paragraphs below find evidence for Jody's moral maturation in "The Great Mountains":]

As the second story, "The Great Mountains," begins, we find that the once-trusting Jody has become cruel and callous. He irrationally tortures a long-suffering dog, and he equally irrationally kills a thrush.When he hides the bird's body to avoid telling the truth, Steinbeck writes, "He didn't care about the bird, or its life, but he knew what the older people would say if they had seen him kill it; he was ashamed of their potential opinion." He is no longer respectful of adults, but he still fears them. He has graduated to that intermediate state between childhood and manhood in which the principal guide to conduct is fear of public opinion, a state beyond which many people, of course, never advance. Like other fearful people, too, Jody has reached a state where he does not wish to accept responsibility. When an old man approaches him, he turns abruptly and runs to the house for help.

This old man is the central figure in the story. He has lived as a child on the land where the ranch stands. He has come home to die now that he is too old to work. Jody's father, who unsympathetically refuses to let him stay, compares him to an old horse "who ought to be shot." Only Jody talks to the old man and learns that he has once visited with his father the great mountains that Jody admires, but the old man remembers nothing of them except that it was "quiet and nice" there. Jody also learns that the old man's most prized possession is a rapier that he has inherited from his father. The next morning both the old man and the superannuated horse to which Jody's father compared him are gone; they have been seen heading towards the the great mountains. Jody discovers that the old man has taken none of his possessions but the rapier. As Jody thinks of the old man, the boy is filled with "a nameless sorrow." This is his recognition that adults, too, are not always to be feared, that they also have their problems, become worn out, useless, unwanted. If youth, as he has learned earlier, has its tragedies, so does old age. His sympathies have been expanded.

—Warren G. French, *John Steinbeck* (Boston: G.K. Hall & Co., 1975): p. 65.

Robert M. Benton on Conflicting Models of Male Adulthood

[Robert M. Benton teaches English at Central Washington State College and has published numerous articles on American literature. Here he contrasts the roles of Carl Tiflin, Jody's father, and Billy Buck, the hired man, as two images of paternal authority in "The Gift":]

Slowly, Steinbeck makes explicit the contrast between Billy and Carl. Billy helps Jody halter-break Gabilan, and Jody learns quickly and well. Steinbeck notes that Jody's work with the halter "approached perfection," but Carl does not praise the boy:

> "He's getting to be almost a trick pony. I don't like trick horses. It takes all the dignity out of a horse to make him do tricks. Why, a trick horse is kind of like an actor—no dignity, no character of his own. I guess you better be getting him used to the saddle pretty soon."

Steinbeck intensifies the contrast between the two men during the pony's illness. Although Billy tries to be optimistic, he never lies to Jody.

> Jody looked unbelieving at Billy Buck. "He's awful sick."
> Billy thought a long time what to say. He nearly tossed off a careless assurance, but he saved himself in time. "Yes, he's pretty sick," he said at last. "I've seen worse ones get well. If he doesn't get pneumonia, we'll pull him through. You stay with him. If he gets worse, you can come and get me."

Carl's approach is completely different. When Jody is depressed, Carl tells him a story about a man who ran naked and had a tail and ears like a horse, and one about brothers who hid a vein of gold so carefully they could never again locate it.

> "Isn't that funny?" he asked.
> Jody laughed politely and said, "Yes, sir."
> His father was angry and hurt, then. He didn't tell any more stories.

Carl cannot sense the depth of his son's emotions, for his mind is on his own feelings, not Jody's.

Perhaps Carl Tiflin is just insensitive, but Steinbeck does not let the reader forget the contrast. After Billy opens the pony's windpipe, Jody goes to work with a swab to keep mucus from closing the breathing hole.

> Jody's father walked into the barn and stood with them in front of the stall. At length he turned to the boy. "Hadn't you better come with me? I'm going to drive over the hill." Jody shook his head. "You better come on, out of this," his father insisted.
>
> Billy turned on him angrily. "Let him alone. It's his pony, isn't it?"
>
> Carl Tiflin walked away without saying another word. His feelings were badly hurt.

One may feel sorrow for a father so unable to understand his son and so incapable of fulfilling his needs, but the fact remains that Billy knows what Jody must have and he is capable of giving it.

The last few lines of "The Gift" complete the picture Steinbeck has drawn. Jody falls asleep and allows the pony to stumble out of the barn. By the time he reaches his pony the buzzards have already commenced their work. In a mad fury Jody grabs a buzzard and beats it mercilessly. "He was still beating the dead bird when Billy Buck pulled him off, and held him tightly to calm his shaking." But why was it Billy who held him and tried to calm him? Why not Carl? All Carl can do is ask Jody if he doesn't know that the buzzard didn't kill the pony.

> It was Billy Buck who was angry. He had lifted Jody in his arms and had turned to carry him home. But he turned back on Carl Tiflin. "'Course he knows it," Billy said furiously, "Jesus Christ! man, can't you see how he'd feel about it?"

And, of course, that is Steinbeck's point. Carl is blind; he hates weakness in others but cannot see it in himself. Jody has grown and accepts his responsibility for the pony's death. But Carl does not understand this. Billy is the natural man who can sense the magnitude of Jody's grief and who alone is capable of the appropriate response.

"The Gift" is a moving story. Its central figure, Jody Tiflin, grows through "loss and acceptance." But it is Billy Buck who guides Jody's education and demonstrates that nobility of character which Steinbeck portrays in his more widely acclaimed fiction.

—Robert M. Benton, "Realism, Growth, and Contrast in 'The Gift,'" *Steinbeck Quarterly* 6, no. 1 (Winter 1973): pp. 8–9.

RICHARD F. PETERSON ON PROFOUND MYSTERIES IN "THE GREAT MOUNTAINS"

[Richard F. Peterson teaches at Southern Illinois University and has written many articles on Steinbeck and full-length studies including *Mary Lavin* (1978) and *William Butler Yeats* (1982) In this excerpt Peterson demonstrates how Jody comes to associate the powerful, unknown, exciting quality of the western mountains with Gitano, an elderly man who has "come home" to die on the Tiflin ranch:]

Jody's own groping search for something more than the empty routine of his present world is suggested initially through his interest in the great mountains. Unlike the mountains of the east, the Gabilans, which Jody associates with life and joviality (the red pony's name was Gabilan), the western mountains, the Great Ones, evoke a sense of wonder and mystery. When each adult Jody questions fails to satisfy his belief in the profundity of the mountains (their explanations range from his father's adult, naturalistic view to the childish fairy tales offered by his mother and Billy Buck), he comes to believe that the mountains are to be both feared and loved. When the ancient Gitano comes "home" to the Tiflin ranch, presumably to die, Jody wastes little time before asking the old man if he comes from the great mountains. This time the adult's response does not betray Jody's feelings. Gitano, whose lean, straight body seems somehow youthful and timeless despite the dried and sunken appearance of the flesh, replies negatively to Jody's question, but he remembers a time when as a child he went into the mountains with his father. Though he has no direct knowledge of the mountains to pass on to the boy, Jody's question stirs something dimly remembered within the old man. Even though Jody learns only that the experience was "nice," he now associates the great mountains with Gitano, who seems to share the boy's inarticulate belief in the great mystery of the mountains and, because of his age and experience, appears to Jody to have a personal, secret awareness of the meaning of the mountains.

The mystery and terror of the great mountains, the strangely timeless quality of Gitano's inner strength, and Jody's innocent yet penetrating questioning, all seem suggestive of a theme broader and deeper in meaning than Jody's discovery of an indifferent nature which frustrates the old and the useless. The barren condition of the land and the fundamental novitiate-priest relationship which begins to form from the conversations between Jody and Gitano also indicate an experience that is spiritual as well as naturalistic. The young boy and the old man seem to share an inarticulate, vaguely conscious desire to realize the human spirit in an otherwise indifferent universe. For Gitano, the wounds suffered in his life have cut deep into the flesh, but the inner fibre of the man is untouched by misfortune and injury. All that remains in life for Gitano is the quiet acceptance of physical death, but in such a way as to justify the preservation of this inner character. Within his naturalistic role as wanderer, he apparently desires to understand his approaching death as the completion of a journey rather than the running down and expiration of the physical man. The mountains evoke not only a sense of the lost innocence and mystery of childhood but also the tradition and authority associated with the father. What Jody seeks is a meaning and purpose behind his entry into life which is compatible with his inner sense of wonder and mystery. His problem, not fully realized within his own mind because of his limited knowledge and experience, is to find an event in the physical world which matches his capacity for belief. In this sense, both the inexperienced boy and the physically exhausted old man are groping their way toward a spiritual meaning in a world which contradicts their awareness of something existent beyond appearance and routine.

—Richard F. Peterson, "The Grail Legend and Steinbeck's 'The Great Mountains,'" *Steinbeck Quarterly* 6, no. 1 (Winter 1973): pp. 11–12.

ROBERT H. WOODWARD ON JODY'S LESSON IN SOCIAL RESPONSIBILITY

[Robert H. Woodward is professor of English and associate dean in the School of Humanities and the Arts at the University of California at San Jose. He edited *The Correspondence of Harold Frederic* (1977). In the excerpt below he outlines Billy Buck's influential lessons in the bittersweet necessity of keeping one's promises and affirming the binding nature of social responsibility:]

But however much Billy cares for Nellie, he is aware of his larger responsibility to Jody. Because of his role in the sickness and death of Gabilan, he is fallible in Jody's eyes and can redeem himself only by seeing that Nellie throws a fine colt for Jody. In some measure, of course, his desire to keep his promise to Jody is selfish, for his reputation as a horseman is again being tested. His private anguish that follows the death of Nellie, however, suggests that were it not for his promise to Jody he would have handled the problem of the birth as any good horseman would have done—by sacrificing the colt to save the mare. In this sense Billy is abandoning the rules, and even jeopardizing his reputation in the eyes of adults, to keep a promise to a boy. His act is one of total selflessness in fulfillment of his sense of responsibility to another human being.

Jody's physical and mental paralysis at the end of the story—after he has heard the hammer crunch Nellie's skull, and watched Billy cut the colt from Nellie's belly, tear the sac with his teeth, and deposit his offering at Jody's feet—comes partly because of the terrible scene he has just witnessed; but, more, "the haunted, tired eyes of Billy Buck hung in the air ahead of him." Jody has his colt. It has cost him peonage for a spring and summer and increased chores for a year. It has cost Billy Buck, however, far more. The story ends with the suggestion that Jody has become dimly aware of what his private desire—his own selfish interest—has cost Billy Buck and that he is confused and humbled by this knowledge. At the beginning of the story Jody is responsible solely to himself; later he is responsible to Nellie for purely personal reasons; at the end comes the possibility of his awareness of his responsibility to other human beings. His world has enlarged; he is a person to whom others are responsible, and he, in turn, is responsible to them for the anguish and pain and sacrifice he himself has caused. His tentative awareness of the interrelationship between human beings is manifested in the following story, "The Leader of the People," through his sympathetic response to his grandfather's definition of "westering." The knowledge that Jody gains is beyond his power to verbalize, but in the following story there is evidence that he has recognized what the events in "The Promise" dramatize—that the human community is made up of individuals who are capable to some degree of subordinating their private, selfish interests to the larger purpose or spirit of the group, or member of that group, as Billy has done for Jody.

The title, emphasizing the *promise,* underscores this concept. Though there are several promises in the story—that of Jody's father to give Jody a colt if he will pay for the service and care for Nellie, those of Jody to honor his contract and behave more responsibly—the central promise is of course Billy's: "There's your colt. I promised. And there it is." It is a promise kept in the face of difficult obstacles, a promise kept only through personal sacrifice. Further, it is a human promise kept when natural promises are unfulfilled. Nellie had thrown fine colts before; she should have again. But nature is unpredictable. Human responsibility need not be. The self-less man, even with pain, can keep his promise and, in his pain, demonstrate the meaning of responsibility and human community.

—Robert H. Woodward, "Steinbeck's 'The Promise,'" *Steinbeck Quarterly* 6, no. 1 (Winter 1973): pp. 17–18.

RICHARD ASTRO ON STEINBECK'S USE OF NON-TELEOLOGICAL THINKING

[Richard Astro has served on the board of *Steinbeck Quarterly* and is active in Steinbeck scholarship. In the early 1970s he was associate professor of English at Oregon State University. *Edward F. Ricketts* (1976) and *John Steinbeck and Edward F. Ricketts: The Shaping of a Novelist* (1981) are among his books. Here he traces the complexity of Steinbeck's representation of Carl Tiflin, Grandfather, and Jody, as per their conformity to Steinbeck and Ricketts' definition of "non-teleological thinking":]

Steinbeck's non-teleological means of viewing life is a highly valu-able tool by which to probe beneath the surface meaning of "The Leader of the People." Ostensibly, as Grommon suggests, Steinbeck seems to be saying that Carl Tiflin is a failure whose cruelty and cowardice are manifest in his unwillingness to listen to Grandfather. Correspondingly, Jody might well be assumed to be Steinbeck's hero, since he seems to emerge into compassionate adulthood when he offers Grandfather the glass of lemonade. And, of course, Steinbeck, through the character of Grandfather, appears to lament the exhaustion of the western frontier, since all that remains of "the big beast" that "carried life out here and set it down the way those ants carry eggs" is "a line of old men along the shore hating the ocean because it stopped them." But these interpretations, while valid to a point, are shallow and incomplete. For Steinbeck, consciously striving to avoid one-sided and blame-assigning readings of his characters' actions, deliberately creates highly complex characters whose acts and attitudes cannot be explained so simply.

Certainly, Carl Tiflin treats Grandfather cruelly. At the same time, however, Steinbeck portrays Carl as an honest man and a good rancher, whose understandable anger over his father-in-law's garrulousness, as Lisca notes, may well represent his resentment at being forced to live an unheroic life. Similarly, Grandfather, the leader of "the big crawling beast" whose face and figure still possess "a granite dignity," is a slow man for whom "every motion seemed an impossible thing." And while his enduring sensitivity suggests that he is not one of those pitiable "old men along the shore" (though he does live there), he is a rigidly inflexible man unable to adapt to modern times. Indeed, for Grandfather, "once made, no step could ever be retraced; once headed in a direction, the path would never bend nor the pace increase nor slow." At the same time, Jody's compassion is born of his juvenile fantasies of adventure which distinctly prohibit him from understanding the true meaning of Grandfather's expression of the unifying aspirations of the "group man." This belief is, of course, central to the thematic core of much of Steinbeck's fiction, and it receives its first explicit expression in Grandfather's insistence that what was important about "westering" was not the Indians nor the adventures that Jody dreams about, but rather the fact of "a whole bunch of people made into one big crawling beast which wanted only westering."

Finally, while there is some evidence to support the thesis that Steinbeck views the modern spirit (symbolized by Jody's mouse hunt) as soft-willed in comparison with the heroic exploits of those men "of a staunchness unknown in this day," most of the sentiments about the grandeur of the past exist only in Jody's mind. Indeed, even Grandfather admits that "hunting Indians and shooting children and burning teepees" really "wasn't much different from your mouse hunt."

And so, while Steinbeck does analyze his characters, and while he does lament the passing of the frontier, his decision to avoid judging these characters and the age in which they live suggests that "The Leader of the People" may actually say somewhat more. In the *Log*, Steinbeck and Ricketts define non-teleological thinking as a *modus operandi*, a method which "extends beyond thinking even to living itself; in fact by inferred definition it transcends the realm of thinking possibilities, it postulates 'living into.'" Thus, in "The Leader of the People," Steinbeck "lives into" life on the Triflin ranch, and he transcends the realm of casual thinking to present a moving account of "something that happened." Unwilling to place the simplistic blinders of right and wrong on the actions and attitudes of his characters, Steinbeck develops a unified field of reality in which he does achieve Whipple's "middle distance." He portrays with a maximum of precision and lucidity, a select group of simple, decent people living and interacting with one another.

Steinbeck's remarks in "The Leader of the People" about the group-man theory, his statements about the pioneer spirit, and his characterizations of Grandfather's nostalgia, Carl's insensitivity, and Jody's compassion are ultimately significant in the way each serves an integral part of a larger, generally objective depiction of human experience. Indeed, Steinbeck's unique ability to move beyond the limits of causes and reasons to "the whole picture" is what gives "The Leader of the People" its particular flavor of excellence.

—Richard Astro, "Something That Happened: A Non-Teleological Approach to 'The Leader of the People,'" *Steinbeck Quarterly* 6, no. 1 (Winter 1973): pp. 22–23.

Plot Summary of
"The Chrysanthemums"

"The Chrysanthemums" dramatizes an afternoon in the life of Elisa Allen, a 35-year-old housewife, and her husband Henry, who live in the Salinas Valley of California. Between two encounters with her husband—his invitation to dinner and a movie to celebrate a successful business deal, and their consequent setting out for town—Elisa converses with a shrewd, attractive repairman passing through on his meandering San Diego to Seattle business route. Their brief interaction provides the story's most intense event, illuminating intriguing aspects of her character and changing her behavior towards her husband.

The story opens with a description of the "grey-flannel fog of winter" encircling the Salinas Valley that creates the appearance of a "closed pot." This stiflingly domestic image is unrelieved by the land's appearance: although the ground seems luminous with promise of warmth and growth, sunshine does not come, and the ground awaits a rainfall which, according to the narrator, is prevented by the fog. The Allen ranch awaits rain, too, showing how the landscape bears the symbolic weight of the estranged couple: it seems productive, but quickly reveals a need for rejuvenation and relief from its isolating, restrictive perfection.

From her fenced-in garden, Elisa watches her husband, Henry, talk to businessmen. We see their transaction, and indeed most of the narrative activity, through her eyes. She doesn't appear interested, returning to work in her garden, where her concentration on the task of uprooting last year's chrysanthemums is steady and her delight and pride in her work implicit. Her garden provides a space in which she creates an ideal of order that borders on the excessive. Her work is "over-eager, over-powerful" and even her oversized, androgynous clothing reveals that she is more capacious and "strong" (an oft-repeated epithet) than her situation allows her to be. Her exceptionally neat appearance reflects personal severity and control, and she creates a sense of physical and emotional distance between herself and her husband. She actively creates a world unto itself that she controls and admires as pure and successful. She wipes out pests before they enter the soil into which she sends her hand,

and this action is as close as she gets to confronting the inevitable, detrimental effects of being in the actual world, since mostly she seems enclosed in her own fantasy life of unchanging beauty.

While she gardens, Henry comes and leans over the fence, offering to take her out to celebrate his business deal. He praises her industriousness, and she takes pride in his compliments. When he leaves, she is suddenly interrupted by the arrival of the repairman and his gangling dog, who encounters the Allen ranch shepherd dogs. She notices that the repairman is large, worn but not aged, and attractively contemplative. After exchanging pleasantries, she aloofly declares she has nothing for repair. By refusing to capitulate to his demands, she retains control, but he deftly shifts the topic to her chrysanthemum bed, noticing that he has tapped the source of Elisa's immense energy and pride. Elisa grows visibly excited as he solicits her planting advice and asks and receives some roots, supposedly on behalf of a nearby woman friend. Like a child's, her eyes widen, and her appearance is described in increasingly erotic tones that suggest a deep, possibly naive, understanding of her own preoccupation with the chrysanthemums. For example, she shakes her hair out from beneath her man's hat, digs a soil base for the seeds with her bare hands instead of using the gloves and trowel she had used before, and moves with a hitherto unprecedented liveliness. She uses blatantly sexual metaphors, comparing pruning her chrysanthemum bushes to feeling the night stars penetrate her body, "hot and sharp and lovely." In an instant her fingers nearly brush against his pants as she obsequiously kneels towards him; this detail, added for the published version of the story in 1938, suggests her unknowingly shameful behavior and marks a crucial turning point in the story.

The sexual symbolism of her position, language, and actions shows the shift in power relations: the repairman has placed Elisa in a vulnerable state, ready to satisfy his desire for money. She finally offers him two pans and fifty cents. Before he leaves, Elisa insists on a woman's equality in making repairs, but by this point his struggle is over and he leaves. She whispers a farewell and enters the house.

Elisa embarks on a ritualistic cleansing of her body in the bath, scouring herself with pumice until turning red. Her attitude while dressing for dinner suggests a newly discovered confidence and pleasure in womanhood, as she chooses her most feminine clothing. In the story's final interaction between Elisa and Henry, the couple seem to behave in ways that are at once mechanistic and inscrutable: she prepares Henry's bath, puts out his clothing, comes to the car—after much delay—and sits beside him as they drive into town. While her actions seem generous, she has also made him wait a long time for her in the car, and she reacts with jumpiness when Henry tells her that she looks nice. Suddenly she sees the parked repairman's vehicle and the chrysanthemum roots she gave him scattered on the ground nearby. At this point Elisa asks for wine at dinner, and Henry is shocked when she suggests that they go to a prize fight (earlier she had rebuffed this request, treating it with frightful seriousness). She finally retreats and renounces her desire to go. The story's abstruse final image is of Elisa crying to herself as they drive to town. Whether she is ashamed or saddened by either her enthusiastic encounter with the repairman, which she has not related to her husband, or the man's disregard for her seeds, remains unclear. ❀

List of Characters in
"The Chrysanthemums"

Elisa Allen is a lean, trim, thirty-five-year-old housewife whose major chore is tending to the gardens surrounding the Salinas Valley home she keeps with her husband Henry. Her activity is insistently described as too small in scope for her capabilities, and she is so attentive to detail that she seems to garden at the expense of other conjugal activities. Her relationship with her husband is mildly affectionate but seems to be filled with many misunderstandings. By contrast, when the repairman visits, she instantly becomes at ease and laughs with him, animating her conversation with advice and jokes. She takes pride in her chrysanthemums, whose size and beauty bring her immoderate pleasure, and her voice becomes sexy as she describes the physical satisfaction she receives from planting. Additionally, grooming herself and feeling confident and feminine take the place of real marital affection. Her activities after the encounter with the repairman suggest that she is alternately ashamed and reawakened by it.

Henry Allen is Elisa Allen's husband. Through her gaze we watch him perform a successful transaction with businessmen. He knows not to disturb her in her garden, and when he asks her to dinner he praises her planting and comes over to, but does not cross, the fence that surrounds her garden. He seems to enjoy her company, is eager to please her, and does not mind her absorption by other preoccupations, yet to an outsider he would seem a rather repressed man. He is otherwise treated well by Elisa, who fixes his bath and lays out his clothes before their outing. The extent of their miscommunication is evident in her questioning of his praise that she looks "nice" and "strong" as well as in his surprise at her knowledge of violent prize fights. He is shrewd enough to notice a transformation in her after she has been with the repairman, and is eager to go out more often, but does not probe the possible reasons for her changed state.

The repairman comes through town on the San Diego to Seattle route. He stops at the Allen ranch to find work and then promises to take chrysanthemum seeds to a neighbor woman. He is a large, older man who does not look as old as he probably is. He seems to have depth to Elisa and intrigues her. Like Henry, he leans over the fence to converse with her and initially is rebuffed, but he skillfully turns the conversation to something that stimulates her: chrysanthemums. He flirts with her, asking leading questions that increasingly excite her interest. Finally he enters the garden, gets pots to mend and earns fifty cents from her. He refuses to admit that women can compete with his skills, and then rushes off, back onto the road. He later discards the chrysanthemum seeds he had been given by Elisa. ✿

Critical Views on
"The Chrysanthemums"

[Mordecai Marcus is a poet and has taught English at the University of Nebraska since 1965. He has published poetry, many articles, and a book entitled *The Poems of Robert Frost: An Explication* (1991). In this excerpt, he analyzes Elisa Allen's vague sexuality, claiming that her femininity is challenged by her husband and her encounter with the repairman:]

Elisa's stance as her husband emerges dressed for the evening out—"Elisa stiffened and her face grew tight"—begins the most difficult sequence in the story. Her action suggests feelings of superiority over her husband, a sudden distaste for someone to whom she must play the woman, and on the deepest level the ambivalence of her desire to be seen as a woman. Her husband's painfully inadequate and puzzled "Why—why Elisa. You look so nice!" suggests that he has not perceived her adequately as a woman, has probably been blind to her needs as a woman. In a complex but brief dialogue, we see him perceive her strength as somehow masculine, to which observation she replies with violent ambivalence, asserting her strength but shocked at the implications that it is masculine. Surely Henry has little understanding of her needs or dilemma.

As Elisa sees her discarded chrysanthemums on the roadway, she reacts at first with an assertion of social norms: "It will be good, tonight, a good dinner," which shows that she is denying her real feelings and pretending that marriage, husbandry, and entertainment are part of a naturally fulfilling cycle. But as she turns from the quest for sensation in wine and in the spectacle of the violent prize fights, to pleasure in the thought of vindictive assault on men, we see that she is reacting to knowledge of her failure. Her feminine self, her capacity for fructification and childbearing have been thoughtlessly tossed aside (just as they have probably been unrecognized by the man at her side), and the power in which she rejoiced is revealed to be a futile substitute for the power of being a woman, which is at the center of her aspirations.

Her sudden interest in the details of the boxing matches suggests many things. In proposing that she attend the fights she is again retreating from her failure as a woman, to an identification with men—the spectators at the fights. But her combination of horror and vindictiveness about the boxers shows a reassertion of her hurt femininity. She dreams of seeing men, who have failed her, punished, and she also wants to punish herself for her failure as a woman. As she abandons her interest in the fights and comforts herself with the thought that wine at dinner will be enough, she accepts her failure to be fully successful as a woman and again comforts herself with a mild symbol of extra-domestic excitement. At the end we see her as a woman, but only that ghost of a woman which nature and society have permitted her to be. She cries like an old woman because she has given in to passivity and potential dessication, though tears like hers are shed by many a young girl.

—Mordecai Marcus, "The Lost Dream of Sex and Childbirth in 'The Chrysanthemums,'" *Modern Fiction Studies* 11, no. 1 (Spring 1965): pp. 57–58.

ELIZABETH E. McMAHAN ON MARITAL MISCOMMUNICATION IN THE STORY

[Elizabeth E. McMahan was an NDEA Fellow at the University of Oregon in 1968–69. In this selection she perceptively discusses the estranged relationship between Elisa Allen and her husband, Henry, through an analysis of their conversations:]

In order to understand Elisa's emotions, we first should look closely at the relationship between her and her husband. Some critics have said it demonstrates confidence and mutual respect. Partially true, certainly, but confidence and mutual respect are not the only qualities that Elisa Allen desires in her marriage. The evidence points to an outwardly passive, comfortable relationship between the two which satisfies Henry completely but leaves Elisa indefinably restless with excessive energy which she sublimates into the "over-eager" cultivation of her chrysanthemums and the care of her "hard-swept looking little house with hard-polished windows." Henry is a good provider, we can be sure; he has just received a good price for thirty head of cattle. He is also thoughtful; he invites his wife to go into town that evening to celebrate the sale. A good provider, a thoughtful husband. But what else? There is a distinct lack of rapport between these two, despite all that mutual respect. And the confidence which some critics observe is an assurance of each other's capability is not a warm mutual confidence of things shared.

We see this lack of rapport demonstrated early in the story as Henry makes a suggestion for their evening's entertainment:

> Henry put on his joking tone. "There's fights tonight. How'd you like to go to the fights?"
> "Oh, no," she said breathlessly. "No, I wouldn't like fights."
> "Just fooling, Elisa. We'll go to a movie."

The fact that husband and wife do not share an interest in sports is not remarkable, but the fact that Elisa responds seriously to Henry's "joking tone" suggests either that she lacks a sense of humor or that for some reason she is not amused by Henry's teasing. We discover later that she has a ready sense of humor when talking to someone other than Henry. Unmistakably, Henry has no gift with words. When he compliments his wife on her chrysanthemums, he praises their size not their beauty and does so in the most prosaic terms. When he wants to compliment his wife on her appearance, he stammers, as if in surprise—and Eliza is hardly elated by the banal adjective:

> "Why—why, Elisa. You look so nice!"
> "Nice? You think I look nice? What do you mean by *nice*?"
> Henry blundered on. "I don't know. I mean you look different, strong and happy."

Henry's word choice here is particularly unfortunate since his wife has just devoted her entire attention to heightening her femininity. She has put on her "newest underclothing and her nicest stockings and the dress which was the symbol of her prettiness." "Strong" is the way she least wants to appear. But Henry manages to make matters even worse. Bewildered by Elisa's sharp retort, he is inspired to his only attempt at figurative language in hopes of making himself clear: "'You look strong enough to break a calf over your knee, happy enough to eat it like a watermelon.'" It is hard to fancy the woman who would be pleased by Henry's agricultural comparison. Elisa is not amused.

—Elizabeth E. McMahan, "'The Chrysanthemums': Study of a Woman's Sexuality," *Modern Fiction Studies* 14, no. 4 (Winter 1968–69): pp. 454–55.

ROY S. SIMMONDS ON ELISA'S QUEST FOR NON-SEXUAL POWER

[Roy S. Simmonds is a formidable Steinbeck scholar and an author of *Steinbeck's Literary Achievement* (1976) and *John Steinbeck: The War Years* (1996). In an article that compares the published story with manuscript versions, he builds a case for Elisa's desire for domination in her human relationships and her lack of sexual feelings towards her husband:]

Most scholars to this date have postulated the theory that Elisa is a similarly frustrated woman, that her husband is unable to satisfy her sexual hunger. It has even been proposed that Henry is impotent. I would however suggest that there is a case for suspecting that Elisa is the one who is unable or unwilling to satisfy her partner sexually. All her sex drive seems to be directed towards the care and propagation of her flowers, the phallic symbols over which she exercises complete mastery. This feeling that Elisa has for her flowers is perhaps more forcibly expressed in the original wording of the "Manuscript B" text, which is reproduced below, rather than it is in the published text. The words in italics represent Steinbeck's above-the-line revisions and/or additions, and the words in parentheses represent deletions.

> *It's* [w]hen you're budding (your mind and your soul and your love) *everything* go[es] right down into your finger tips. You watch your fingers work (and) [word illegible] you can feel (the joy in them) *how it is.*

Elisa's carelessness in the matter of her everyday attire, her obvious reluctance to accept the fact of her femininity—exemplified by the manner in which she scrubs her body after the tinker has left (perhaps an over-reaction to his comment that his sort of existence was not "the right kind of life for a woman" as well as being the symbolic act of purification it is popularly accepted to represent) and by the belligerent manner in which she over-reacts to her husband's surprised comment on how "nice" she looks dressed up for the trip to Salinas—indicates a personality who rejects the submissive female role, who even finds the act of love wholly distasteful and to be avoided whenever possible. "I'm strong," she boasts to Henry. "I never knew before how strong."

In the published version of the story we are given very little information about Henry. Not even the merest mention is made of his physical appearance. He remains a shadowy figure throughout the story and because of his indistinctness it is possible to regard him more sympathetically than the Henry of "Manuscript A." He is patently the weaker of the two personalities, as indeed he is unequivocally presented in "Manuscript A." In that first version, as we have seen, Elisa rejoices in her sense of dominance over her husband. Whilst I would agree that there could be considerable dangers in linking characterizations drawn in that first version with the protagonists as presented in "Manuscript B" and the published version, I would nevertheless submit that Elisa's behavior in "Manuscript A" goes some way toward explaining much of her behavior in the published version. The manner in which she mocks her husband when he compliments her upon her appearance and her perverse action in keeping him waiting while she puts on her coat, forcing him to idle the car motor, and then going out the moment he switches off the motor have tended to be regarded as simply her reaction to the tinker's visit and a manifestation of the feeling of discontent he has engendered in her. To my mind, however, these actions are more indicative of what is probably the normal pattern of Elisa's and Henry's married life.

Elisa's need for this sense of dominance over the male is not confined solely to her feelings towards her husband. She experiences this need to assert her superiority over all men, contriving always to keep them at arm's length. Her flower garden is surrounded by a protective wire fence ostensibly to keep out animals, but the fence also serves to exclude her husband and the tinker. It is not until the tinker has verbally seduced her with his assumed interest in her chrysanthemums and is admitted to her side of the fence that Elisa finds her defenses in danger of collapsing to the extent that she almost allows herself to succumb to male dominance. Almost, but not quite. "Kneeling there, her hand went toward his legs in the greasy black trousers. Her hesitant fingers almost touched the cloth. Then her hand dropped to the ground. She crouched low like a fawning dog." When eventually she rises to her feet there is a look of shame on her face. Again, the general interpretation has been that her shame is the shame of a married woman briefly tempted by thoughts of a possible clandestine sexual adventure. I would alternatively suggest that her shame is the shame of a woman who realizes that she has momentarily lowered her defenses and all but offered herself to the male dominance she so greatly despises. It is significant that for all the sexually-charged atmosphere that exists between Elisa and the tinker during the short time of his visit they never at any point make actual physical contact. She does not touch his trousered legs. She does admittedly hand him the flowerpot and the two saucepans and takes the saucepans back from him, but there would be no touching of hands in doing this. When she comes to pay him, she avoids physical contact by dropping the fifty cent piece into his hand.

Apart from the one little lapse, Elisa maintains, at least in her own mind, her dominance over the tinker. When the man first arrives, she deprecates (in semi-humorous fashion) the prowess of his dog and then of his mismatched team of horses. Later she insists that she would be equal to living his rough open-air life with all that it entails, and finally she challenges his own prowess, claiming that she could sharpen scissors and mend pots just as efficiently, if not better, than he.

—Roy S. Simmonds, "The Original Manuscript of Steinbeck's 'The Chrysanthemums'," *Steinbeck Quarterly* 7, no. 3/4 (Summer-Fall 1974): pp. 107–9.

CHARLES A. SWEET JR. ON THE REJECTION OF ELISA BY MEN AND SOCIETY

[Charles A. Sweet Jr. received his Ph.D. from Florida State University, where his dissertation was entitled *Bernard*

Malamud and the Use of Myth (1970). He has taught at Eastern Kentucky University and has published short stories and poetry in addition to essays in the Colby Library Quarterly. In this excerpt Sweet discusses Elisa's failure both to conduct a successful business transaction and to become more than an undesirable sexual object:]

Even before Elisa can discern the true shape of the dark speck, she knows what she has already unconsciously assimilated. In her business deal, which is the truest test of her desired equality, she has been less successful than her husband. Where Henry has received almost his price for the cattle, Elisa has received nothing for her chrysanthemum seeds. Instead she has paid the fixer fifty cents to perform a task she admittedly could do. She has failed to communicate with the fixer as he has taken her pot and thrown away the chrysanthemum seeds; more importantly he has stripped her of her dignity and dreams of equality. And finally when he was faced with a fawning, sexually aroused woman, he rejected her for that, too. Elisa cannot even take refuge in her basic sexual femininity. And so she is even further reduced to the wife whose hard work is rewarded simply with a token Saturday night out. She accepts this lesser role by mentioning "It will be good tonight, a good dinner." Her desires for revenge are useless as she doesn't even want to go to the fights. And in the end her dreams of feminine equality are so shattered that her former state is impossible; she accepts her social role and turns the corner at thirty-five; now she is only "an old woman."

Mordecai Marcus, trying to negate the feminism in the story, has commented it is "unthinkable that he [Steinbeck] was suggesting that woman's role must be passive. . . ." Yet, that is exactly what a close analysis of "The Chrysanthemums" reveals. Elisa Allen is no Myra Breckinridge wishing to be Myron but instead the representative of the feminist ideal of equality and its inevitable defeat. The point of the story is not, as previous critics have stressed, that Elisa possesses an unfulfilled sexual need, but rather that the feminist is still a woman and women are fundamentally emotional, as evidenced by tears or sexual arousal. Whereas a man can function unemotionally in the masculine business world and receive nearly his own price, a woman soon operates at less than a rational level and is victimized both by her basic nature and by others. There is nothing to suggest that Elisa's relationship with Henry is sexually inadequate. But a woman has other dimensions than the sexual.

However, for Steinbeck, a masculine-dominated society has so conditioned a female's basic emotional response that in such situations it is inevitably released. Thus, the fixer is only generically guilty. Moreover Elisa's frustration is compounded by being faced with an unfamiliar situation: a male has aroused her but does not want her—she has become a pure object. Though not to the degree of Hemingway, Steinbeck's world is a man's world, a world that frustrates even minor league women's liberationists.

—Charles A. Sweet Jr., "Ms. Elisa Allen and Steinbeck's 'The Chrysanthemums'," *Modern Fiction Studies* 20, no. 2 (Summer 1974): pp. 213–14.

ERNEST W. SULLIVAN ON THE STORY'S THREE HUMAN-CANINE COMPARISONS

[Ernest W. Sullivan has been Associate Professor of English at Texas Tech University, edited Conrad's *Lord Jim,* and has also published *The Influence of John Donne* and a facsimile edition of *The First and Second Dalhousie Manuscripts: Poems and Prose by John Donne and Others.* In this highly astute reading of canine imagery in the story, he unveils striking similarities between the characters and the story's dogs:]

Anyone reading John Steinbeck's "The Chrysanthemums" cannot help being struck by the repeated association of unpleasant canine characteristics with the otherwise attractive Elisa Allen. These associations identify her with the visiting tinker's mongrel dog, further suggesting a parallel between the Allen's two ranch shepherds and the tinker and Elisa's husband, Henry. The correspondences between people and dogs elucidate the social and sexual relationsips of the three humans, as well as foreshadow and explain Elisa's failure at the end of the story to escape from her unproductive and sterile lifestyle.

The dog imagery related to Elisa is uncomplimentary. In her garden, she destroys unpleasant creatures such as "aphids," "bugs," "snails," "cutworms," and similar "pests" with her "terrier fingers." When aroused by the tinker, she "crouched low like a fawning dog." Finally, in response to the tinker's assertion that his life of freedom "ain't the right kind of life for a woman," she bares her teeth in hostile fashion: "Her upper lip raised a little, showing her teeth." Burrowing in flower gardens, fawning, snarling—not a very pleasant picture of man's best friend.

The last two images directly link Elisa to the tinker's mongrel, and their physical descriptions clearly parallel these two unfortunates. She kneels before the tinker like a dog would to shake hands: "Kneeling there, her hand went out toward his legs in the greasy black trousers. Her hesitant fingers almost touched the cloth. Then her hand dropped to the ground. She crouched low like a fawning dog." As Elisa bared her teeth in resistance to the tinker, so his mongrel resisted the two Allen ranch shepherds "with raised hackles and bared teeth." Additionally, the cur is "lean and rangy"; Elisa is "lean and strong." Finally, of course, the tinker's mongrel, unlike the ranch shepherds, contains a mixture of dog breeds, and Elisa's personality mixes masculine and feminine elements.

Whereas Elisa shares several characteristics with the cur, the tinker and Henry resemble the two ranch shepherds. The two shepherds were born to their jobs, which they perform instinctively. Confident that "pots, pans, knives, sisors, lawn mores" can all be "fixed," the tinker feels at home in his occupation and world: "I ain't in any hurry, ma'am. I go from Seattle to San Diego and back every year. Takes all my time. About six months each way. I aim to follow nice weather." Henry Allen is also successful at his job and derives satisfaction from it: "I sold those thirty head of three-year-old steers. Got nearly my own price, too." On the other hand, Elisa, like the mongrel, does not participate in the main work on which her livelihood depends, even though her husband suggests that she should become useful: "I wish you'd work out in the orchard and raise some apples that big." Both Elisa and the cur are merely companions for their respective breadwinners, their subservient position suggested by Elisa's kneeling before the tinker: "She was kneeling on the ground looking up at him."

The interaction of the three dogs closely parallels that of the three people and foreshadows Elisa's eventual failure to escape her confined lifestyle. When the mongrel darts from its accustomed position beneath the tinker's wagon, the two ranch dogs shepherd it back. The mongrel considers fighting, but, aware that it could not overcome the two dogs secure on their home ground, retreats angrily back under the wagon and protection of its owner: "The rangy dog darted from between the wheels and ran ahead. Instantly the two ranch shepherds flew out at him. Then all three stopped, and with stiff and quivering tails, with taut straight legs, with ambassadorial dignity, they slowly circled, sniffing daintily. . . . The newcomer dog, feeling out-numbered, lowered his tail and retired under the wagon with raised hackles and bared teeth."

—Ernest W. Sullivan II, "The Cur in 'The Chrysanthemums,'" *Studies in Short Fiction* 16, no. 3 (Summer 1979): pp. 215–16.

STANLEY RENNER ON SEXUAL DISAPPOINTMENT IN THE STORY'S LAST SECTION

[Stanley Renner publishes on Steinbeck in *Steinbeck Quarterly* and during the past decade has taught as associate professor of English at Illinois State University in Normal, Illinois. His extremely valuable analysis of the story uses previous feminist views in order to show Steinbeck's underlying representation of male sexual dissatisfaction. In this excerpt, Renner examines Elisa's rejection of real versus romanticized sexuality in the last section of the story:]

The last movement of the story, as Elisa and Henry bathe, dress, and set out for Salinas, reveals the outcome of Henry's courtship of his wife. Elisa's savage excoriation of her body as she bathes is usually understood as self-punishment for her fantasized unfaithfulness to Henry with the tinker. But even more pertinently it dramatizes her sexual ambivalence—not the conflict between masculine and feminine impulses within her but between her glowing biological sexuality and her deep aversion to the earthy and animalistic realities of sexual life. In the scene Steinbeck sets up an ironic counterpoint between a beauty magazine stereotype of the lovely woman bathing and dressing for a romantic evening and Elisa's ambivalent behavior. Instead of soaking langorously in her beauty bath, sensuously laving her delicate skin with fragrant feminine soap, she furiously attacks her body with harsh abrasive soap—Lava, perhaps. Dressing for the evening, she puts on clothing that emphasizes her sex appeal. She even puts on "her newest underclothing and her nicest stockings," an act of forethought that can only mean her awareness of the sexual implications of the evening, and pencils her eyebrows and rouges her lips like a courtesan. Yet when her husband comes to the house, instead of responding with the warm glow of romantic anticipation that these preparations imply, she "set herself for Henry's arrival."

Although in body she is outside the fence, throughout this entire movement Elisa continues to erect barriers against her husband's courtship. As Henry hurries to get ready, she awaits him "primly and stiffly," her lack of romantic warmth underscored by the "frosted leaves," "high grey fog," "thin band of sunshine," and general Hardyesque neutral tones of "the grey afternoon" and the landscape in which "she sat unmoving" and unseeing. When Henry appears, she "stiffened and her face grew tight." Surprised and pleased by his wife's attractiveness, because she usually dresses to hide her sex appeal and thus to avoid activating his libido, Henry allows himself a surge of hopeful anticpation to Elisa's unusual display of sexual attractiveness. But emotionally she is still inside her fence; she bristles with wiry defensiveness. Getting mixed signals from this cold, stiff woman dressed to excite his sexual admiration, Henry naturally "looked bewildered. 'You're playing some kind of a game,' he said helplessly." Having stifled his ardent response to her sex appeal, Elisa now reasserts her strong control over the relationship, which resumes its usual course, and Henry gets his emotion under control again: "When he brought his eyes back to her, they were his own again."

This scene, showing Elisa turning away from her husband's courtship, dramatizes what is wrong with the Allens' marriage and answers the story's central question: why is Elisa's life unfulfilled? Steinbeck concludes the scene with what may be a trifle too much ingenuity.

Elisa went into the house. She heard Henry drive to the gate and idle down his motor, and then she took a long time to put on her coat. She pulled it here and pressed it there. When Henry turned the motor off, she slipped into her coat and went out. Perhaps only now, concerned with conserving gasoline, are we struck by this curious and wasteful stalling. But it reveals how Elisa controls Henry's sexual interest in her: she keeps clear of him until his passion, awakened by her sex appeal, has cooled—until he idles down *his* motor and turns it off. Although he passes over the pointed sexual implications of the passage, Roy S. Simmonds observes that this behavior is likely "indicative of what is probably the normal pattern of Elisa's and Henry's married life."

—Stanley Renner, "The Real Woman Inside the Fence in 'The Chrysanthemums,'" *Modern Fiction Studies* 31, no. 2 (Summer 1985): pp. 312–13.

C. KENNETH PELLOW ON HOW THE STORY REPRESENTS LOVING ONE'S WORK

[C. Kenneth Pellow edited, with Alexander Blackburn, *Higher Elevations: Stories from the West* (1993). He is associate professor of English at the University of Colorado, Colorado Springs. In this excerpt he notices the transformations that Elisa and the repairman undergo when immersed in their favorite work:]

Throughout "The Chrysanthemums" there runs a mechanical-and organic contrast that also underscores Elisa's situation. She concentrates nearly all of her time and energy on raising flowers, while it becomes clear to her that it is in the mechanical world that one finds wealth, power, and, most important, self-determination. So, when Henry negotiates with the meat-packers who eventually buy his cattle, all three stand "by the tractor shed, each man with one foot on the side of the little Fordson." And near the end of the story, after Henry has been mildly chastised by Elisa for his "calf" metaphor and had been confronted by her boast of how "strong" she is, he "looked down toward the tractor shed, and when he brought his eyes back to her, they were his own again."

Part of Elisa's ultimate disenchantment with the tinker comes from much the same kind of opposition. This is not at first noticeable, at least to Elisa, for she and the tinker seem more alike than different. They are able, as noted earlier, to share a joke, and Elisa is taken by his ability to turn a poetic phrase, as in his likening of chrysanthemums to "a quick puff of colored smoke." And both are transported when in the midst of what they love doing. Thus Elisa explains to the tinker about "planting hands." I will quote the entire speech, for, within the context of this story, it is a unique passage:

> "Well, I can only tell you what it feels like. It's like when you're picking off the buds you don't want. Everything goes right down into your fingertips. You watch your fingers work. They do it themselves. You can feel how it is. They pick and pick the buds. They never make a mistake. They're with the plant. Do you see? Your fingers and the plant. You can feel that, right up your arm. They know. They never make a mistake. You can feel it. When you're like that you can't do anything wrong. Do you see that? Can you understand that?"

Steinbeck here creates Elisa's breathlessness by deviating from the story's normal style. These eighteen sentences (only one is fragmentary) average less than six words each; none is longer than ten words. In a more typical paragraph of this story—the first, for instance—sentences run up to thirty words or more in length, and average twenty-three. Even in dialogue, syntax is not this terse; in Elisa's last speech before the one quoted above, sentences range up to twenty words in length and average over ten. Immediately after this speech, it becomes even clearer that the breathlessness is sexual, for Elisa proceeds into the speech that ends, "Why you rise up and up! Every pointed star gets driven into your body. It's like that. Hot and sharp and—lovely." As Elizabeth McMahan observes, "The sexual implications of her last four sentences are unmistakable." Steinbeck enforced those implications when he revised the story, as he added the last three sentences.

As Elisa is transported when working with her flowers, so is the tinker when he performs his favorite work. When Elisa has decided that she does, after all, have some work he can do for her, "His manner changed. He became professional." His gear set up, he goes to work at removing dents from her kettles: "His mouth grew sure and knowing. At a difficult part of the work he sucked his under-lip." But there are differences, of course, between the kinds of work that they do. His is with things mechanical and profitably remunera-tive; hers is with things organic and, financially, at least, profitless. It is all too typical of "woman's work." And that she is prohibited from participation in the other kind of work is emphasized by the tinker's observation that his profession "ain't the right kind of life for a woman." Elisa interprets this, probably accurately, as more prohibi-tive than protective. She says as she pays him for his work: "You might be surprised to have a rival some time. I can sharpen scissors, too. And I can beat the dents out of little pots. I could show you what a woman might do." The tinker represents more than sexual disillusionment to (and for) Elisa; he is also the enemy—the repre-sentative of the mechanical, self-reliant fraternity that keeps her in her "place."

—C. Kenneth Pellow, "'The Chrysanthemums' Revisited," Steinbeck Quarterly 22, no. 1/2 (Winter-Spring 1989): pp. 11–13.

DAVID LEON HIGDON ON ELISA AS A MAENAD

[David Leon Higdon has written concordances for novels by Henry James and Conrad and is author of *Time and English Fiction* (1977) and *Shadows of the Past in Contemporary British Fiction* (1985). His essay is a learned and fascinating comparison of Elisa to a semi-triumphant Maenad with the strength to destroy her Dionysian husband:]

In the crucial scene between husband and wife, Elisa sends a most paradoxically mixed message to Henry. On the one hand, she looks "nice" and "happy," an extension of her subservient passivity when "her hesitant fingers" almost touched the tinker's "greasy black trousers" or when she "crouched low like a fawning dog." She has transformed her workaday self into a sex object but could as easily be the manipulative temptress as the docile toy. She does savor this role for a few moments, letting Henry idle the car while she puts on her hat and coat. Peter Lisca has concluded that Elisa has begun a "silent rebellion against the passive role required of her as a woman," and it does indeed appear that she has fired the opening shots in a sexual row by overemphasizing her femininity. On the other hand, Elisa strikes Henry as being "strong." She even boasts, "I'm strong . . . I never knew before how strong," a comment ironically exploded when she shrinks from the symbolic implications of the chrysanthemums in the road. She reads the clump of roots and earth as the tinker's rejection of her inner, true self and his affirmation that her "worthwhile" self is her utilitarian being, symbolized by the pot he keeps. Her logic cannot be faulted because just such a rejection has come earlier in the day when Henry suggests that she could put her "planter's hands" to more "profitable" use on the farm.

If the identification of the allusion embedded in Henry's metaphor is correct, Elisa has encountered Dionysus in disguise, a fact we are asked to recognize in retrospect, precisely the reaction Steinbeck wished to effect. The allusion ties in nicely with the topic of repression, because, as E. R. Dodds argues, "To resist Dionysus is to repress the elemental in one's own nature; the punishment is the sudden complete collapse of the inward dykes when the elemental breaks through perforce and civilisation vanishes." Of course, the elemental in Elisa neither resists nor fully breaks through; rather, the tinker's discarding of her, leaving her the weak and highly secondary revenge of imagining for one moment the physical injury and blood of prize fights and anticipating a meek participation in Dionysus' rites by drinking wine at dinner. "It will be enough," she tells Henry. Unable to vent her anger directly against the rational, practical, and dominant male world and unable to become a true Maenad, the extent of her failure is finally measured by Henry's metaphor.

Has Elisa been totally defeated? Although Charles A. Sweet, Jr. has viewed her as "an embryonic feminist," critical opinion has not been sharply divided. Most critics have seen her as both frustrated and defeated. Tetsumaro Hayashi characterizes the story as "a woman's futile attempt to compensate for a disappointing marriage"; Roy Simmonds sees her tears as "the tears of a bitter, defeated woman"; and Mordecai Marcus, writing about Elisa's "pervasive combination" fusing the masculine and the feminine, concludes that "she is denying her real feelings and pretending the marriage, husbandry, and entertainment are part of a naturally fulfilling cycle." Ernest W. Sullivan has cleverly demonstrated, through a study of the dog imagery, that the "positions of the dogs after the meeting between Elisa and the tinker foreshadow her final defeat." The ending may be more problematic than these critics have argued. The encounter and her reaction will have changed her for the better if, like her chrysanthemum buds, Elisa has only been "plucked," but for the worse if she has been "cut back" too far in an inappropriate season. In either instance, she knows that for a few brief hours she has been one with the worshippers of Dionysus, strong enough to rip the living flesh from a bull, but ultimately unable to free herself from the world she, society, and the Depression have conspired to build around her. Unfortunately, though, the Maenad allusion which richly contextualizes Elisa does not solve the problems of the ending.

—David Leon Higdon, "Dionysian Madness in Steinbeck's 'The Chrysanthemums'," *CML* 11 (Fall 1990): pp. 64–65.

JOHN H. TIMMERMAN ON THE LIVELY ATTRACTION OF OPPOSITES

[John H. Timmerman teaches at Calvin College, Grand Rapids, Michigan and is author of *John Steinbeck's Fiction: The Aesthetics of the Road Taken* (1986) and *The Dramatic Landscape of Steinbeck's Short Fiction* (1990). This excerpt from the latter book discusses how the repairman acts as an opposing outlet for Elisa's intensity:]

Compulsively orderly and neat, Elisa has regimented her bursting creativity into rituals. While Steinbeck deleted the passage recounting her scholastic achievements, he retains her fierce eagerness in a more subtle imagery pattern allied with her gardening. She exudes energy. Her work with the scissors is rapacious, "over-eager, over-powerful." Her "terrier fingers" probe the flower stems with sureness and skill. Yet, for all her energy, her life is very much like the valley itself on this cloudy December day, "a closed pot."

In the story Elisa receives two contrary pulls from outside forces upon her energy. One emanates from the Tinker, who stands as her personal and physical opposite. Languid and disheveled, the Tinker poses a host of polarities to Elisa. While her body looks "blocked and heavy in her gardening costume," the Tinker slouches like a lean rail in a spindly fence. Her powerful force is frequently depicted in masculine terms—"handsome," "strong"—while the Tinker is effeminately deferential. Her energy is opposed by the Tinker's sad, melancholy disposition. Her eyes are "clear as water"; the Tinker's are "dark and full of brooding." She works with living things; he with inanimate objects. Her dog is a lively ranch shepherd; the Tinker's a "lean and rangy mongrel dog." She sports a yellow print dress; he a black suit worn to threads. Elisa's plants stand in soldierly rows of exuberant health; his horse and donkey "drooped like unwatered flowers."

The elaborate but artistically well-hidden list of juxtapositions function ironically, for this disheveled panhandler is also a master con man who manages to probe the heart of Elisa's need in a way that her husband can never approach. He carries with him, beside the reek of long days on the road, the unqualified freedom to follow that road where he wills, his only aim "to follow nice weather." Freedom is the dream he brings.

Despite a keen awareness from the very start that the Tinker is a shyster, Elisa bows to the manipulation as she senses it opens on freedom. Her flowers have been her life, her children, her talent. Her gift is "planting hands," the chrysanthemums her offspring. When the Tinker acknowledges her gift, admitting its dangerous reality, Elisa reveals more of herself—physically and psychologically. She removes her hat and shakes out her long hair, removing layers of repressed desires from her soul. The unmasking comes to a climax, artistic as well as sexual, when she kneels before him to hand him one of her flowers. They are her progeny, her true and secret self. The sexual overtones of the passage are clear. Elisa exclaims, "I've never lived as you do, but I know what you mean. When the night is dark—why, the stars are sharp-pointed, and there's quiet. Why, you rise up and up! Every pointed star gets driven into your body. It's like that. Hot and sharp and—lovely."

—John H. Timmerman, *The Dramatic Landscape of Steinbeck's Short Stories* (Norman, Okla.: University of Oklahoma Press, 1990): pp. 173–75.

JAY PARINI ON THE INFLUENCES OF GARDENING AND D. H. LAWRENCE

[Jay Parini graduated from Lafayette College in 1970 and currently is a professor of English at Middlebury College. He has written *Theodore Roethke: An American Romantic* (1979), edited numerous collections of poetry, and is a prolific poet. He recently published *John Steinbeck: A Biography* (1995). His high praise for Steinbeck's achievement in this story presents helpful literary and biographical clues for understanding Steinbeck's craft, particularly the influence of D. H. Lawrence:]

The opening story, "The Chrysanthemums," sets the tone for the book. It is a brilliant piece of writing, perhaps the best story Steinbeck ever wrote. In it we follow a brief period in the life of a woman, Elisa Allen, who is married to a dull but well-intentioned farmer. Steinbeck writes: "The high grey-flannel fog of winter closed off the Salinas Valley from the sky and from all the rest of the world." As in much of his fiction, this story opens with a personified landscape, a *paysage moralisé* in which the weather and geographical setting are deeply symbolic, gesturing in the direction of the story's ultimate meaning. Here, for instance, the claustrophobic world of Elisa Allen is signaled by the claustrophobic clouds pressing in on the valley. This frustrated woman will never break free.

The title of the story, as well as the theme, reflects again the author's interest in Lawrence (whose first published story was "Odor of Chrysanthemums"). For example, both writers seem to fasten intently on the idea that a new consciousness is growing under, or within, the old rotten one, and that the old must be sacrificed to the new; the apocalyptic flavor of Lawrence is rare in Steinbeck, who might be seen as a "cooler" writer, but they share an urgent belief that one version of civilization has come to an end and the artist must play a key role in developing the new one.

"The Chrysanthemums" is partly about the way Elisa's dreams are manipulated by a passing rogue—a man who repairs household goods. (Steinbeck's fiction is full of men like this one: there is Mac, for instance, from *In Dubious Battle*, who will do anything to win the migrant workers' confidence.) The repairman plays upon Elisa's feelings, pretending to sympathize with her love of flowers, which is all-consuming. Her passion for chrysanthemums in particular symbolizes her intimacy with the rhythms of the natural world and represents her most essential self. Only an author who was himself a gardener could have written about the process of gardening so eloquently:

> "There was a little square sandy bed kept for rooting the chrysanthemums. Wih her trowel she turned the soil over and over, and smoothed it and patted it firm. Then she dug ten parallel trenches to receive the sets. Back at the chrysanthemum bed she pulled out the crisp little shoots, trimmed off the leaves of each one with her scissors and laid it on a small orderly pile."

Steinbeck understands the metaphor of gardening in a deeply symbolic way, using this knowledge to make his point. Elisa is finally hurt by the repairman, who was merely toying with her, but she is not broken, as Charlotte Hadella notes: "Even though, in the end, she thinks of herself as a weak, old woman, the powerful imagery of the strong, new crop of chrysanthemums waiting for rain still dominates the story." She compares Elisa's disappointment to a kind of "pruning—the clipping back of the romantic 'shoots' of her imagination before they can bud so that her energy can feed a strong reality and produce large, healthy blooms."

—Jay Parini, *John Steinbeck: A Biography* (New York: Henry Holt and Co., 1995): pp. 209–11.

Plot Summary of
"The White Quail"

"The White Quail," like "The Chrysanthemums," concerns an estranged couple, the effects on the relationship from the wife's obsession with her gardening activities and, similarly, her increasingly strong identification not only with her garden but especially an object in it. Mary Teller's bonding with the white quail signals her deep desire to remove herself from a painful confrontation with physical reality and its concomitant destructive forces of change, loss, and death. She explicitly regards her garden as herself, and organizes its contents to reflect that identity. Mary insists on the static, bird-friendly, and permanent nature of the garden. She is ruthless about chasing away pests from the garden and ends up also chasing away her husband, Harry, by locking their bedroom door.

A constrictive domestic space is described at the beginning of "The White Quail": the specially designed living room window out of which, from the right perspective, the garden and its surrounding bucolic wilds can be properly seen. The garden is circled by oak trees around which cinerarias grow; in its center is a heart-shaped bird-bath. At the lawn's edge masculine fuchsias stand guard, as if to shield the garden from the encroaching wilderness. Mary's dream of creating this garden was so central that it dominated her choice of a spouse, and she actually believed that it was the garden and not herself that was choosing him. When Harry E. Teller entered their symbiotic lives, the garden was agreeable, and he reacted reassuringly to her ambitions for its construction. He considered her preoccupation with the garden adorable and attractive, blissfully unaware of her lack of reciprocal desire when she let him kiss her.

While she thinks of the garden as inextricably bound up in her sense of self, Harry, of course, thinks of her differently—*like* her garden, but not as if she were the garden. Eventually, it is the gap between her identity with the garden and his noting of what is happening that causes his mounting alienation from her. However, he still does not fully comprehend the strange bond between his wife and her garden. Harry thinks her enthusiasm for the garden shows that she exudes confidence, but she repeatedly expresses insecurity. He finds her personification of the garden's inhabitants endearing and takes satisfaction in their nightly ritual of violently killing pests; this task is their only mutually satisfying activity, a dramatically performed substitute for physical intimacy. Mary is so consumed by the idea of resisting change of any kind that she refuses to let slugs, fallen leaves, or dead plants exist in the garden. Clearly, her interest lies not in creating a productive, natural environment, but in maintaining an impossible dream. When Harry suggests, for example, that a cat's presence might be inhibiting birds from visiting the pool, she immediately wants to kill it with poisoned fish. For her, the pool is a sanctuary in the midst of chaos, a response to the inevitable vulnerability of being human.

Preserving the sanctuary is a daunting task, and the more she tries the more she separates herself from Harry. One night she retrieves scissors from the garden and fantasizes that only her "essence" left the house, while her body stayed in the chair, and she looks back to admire her own poise and prettiness. We learn that her preferred time of day to tend the garden is late afternoon: birds visit, Harry leaves her undisturbed, and she narcissistically imagines conversations between two selves enjoying the garden and the vision of the birds finding safety by the pool. By eventually "becoming" the white quail, Mary merges with the most delicate, ethereal inhabitant of the garden, and identifies with the very vulnerability she refuses to accept, referring to the quail as her "essence," or "secret" self.

A possible motivation for her strong desire to protect the white quail from harm is suggested in the memory of her father. In a brief recollection of their relationship, she remembers receiving packages from Italy in which he sent candy that she "ecstatically" looked at but was not allowed to eat, and later being told of her father's death. These memories may indicate that her mother did not want Mary to fall in love with her father through eating the sweets, or that the candy's taste would have disappointed her, but in either case Mary associates the quail with the "ecstasy" of looking at but not directly experiencing the intense pleasures and pains of food and a loved one's death.

She denies Harry access to her bedroom, locking its door each night and leading the reader to believe the marriage is not even consummated. With the same persistency, Harry still tries opening it. In the story's last scene, Mary spots a cat in the garden, goes into shock, and asks Harry to kill it. When he refuses to do so, she gets another headache like the one prompted by his earlier enthusiasm for a puppy who she imagined might wreak havoc on the garden. She tells him of the white quail in order to win him over, but he still refuses, and in the morning he sets out to stun the cat with his air gun but instead, identifying momentarily with the cat, he shoots the white quail. He cries out, ashamed of himself, "Oh Lord, I'm so lonely!" ❀

List of Characters in
"The White Quail"

Mary Teller is Harry E. Teller's wife. Her character is centered around her intense passion for keeping her garden predator-free, the driving force of her life. Her desire has horrible consequences on her marriage, since the more she thinks of her essence as outside herself and in the garden, the less she can relate to her husband. She spends most of her time in the garden, making sure that it shows no sign of decay or loss. She admires her husband insofar as he complies with her plan, and when he does not, she gets severe headaches. Her resistance to emotional, physical, and especially sexual experience is palpable; she is physically unaffectionate but mildly tolerates his kisses. Mary fantasizes that two selves exist, as if to maximize her pleasure from the garden. One day, she identifies with the white quail she discovers in the garden and believes it her "center" or "heart." When a cat threatens its existence, she frantically insists that her husband kill it, and oddly locks the door after he leaves to stun it.

Harry E. Teller is Mary's husband. Before and at the start of their marriage, he regards Mary's obsession with the garden as charming, but soon becomes frightened by the extent of her identification with it and holds her at a distance, fearing that she isolates herself from him. He takes pride in her chattiness about the garden when they have guests, and joins her in the task of hunting down pests, which brings him inordinate satisfaction. He tries to open her constantly locked door each night, and feels shame at his own desire. He is denied the chance to have a puppy because of its potential effects on the garden. Although for much of the story he is incredibly self-effacing to the point of annihilation, he takes a stand towards the end when he refuses to kill the cat who appears in the garden, only agreeing to stun it with an air gun. His mounting sexual frustration causes him to kill the quail with whom Mary has identified her "essence" instead of harming the cat. The cat can be associated, in this reading, with the male sexual threat that Harry poses to the virginal Mary. After killing the quail, it dawns on Harry that perhaps he has also killed any chance of reconciliation with Mary. ❀

Critical Views on
"The White Quail"

MARILYN MITCHELL ON MARY TELLER'S
UNATTAINABLE PERFECTION

[Marilyn Mitchell received her Ph.D. in history from the University of Kansas and was assistant professor of Humanities at Wayne State University before earning her law degree. Her articles can be found in *Midwest Quarterly, Signs, Southwest Review,* and *Wayne Law Review.* In this excerpt from an article on Steinbeck's strong female characters, she chronicles both Mary Teller's obsession with her garden's mirroring an ideal of unchanging, nurturing existence and her husband's estranged, weak marital position:]

Harry, of course, has no understanding of Mary's personality or motivations, nor does he believe any is necessary. Just as she is attracted to him for his passivity and his income, so he is attracted to her for her apparent delicacy and beauty: "You're so pretty. You make me kind of—hungry." Her attractiveness will also make her an asset to his business: "He was proud of her when people came to dinner. She was so pretty, so cool and perfect." And since he does not expect a pretty girl to have any dimension but the physical, the firm determination with which she engineers the garden's construction comes as a surprise to him: "Who could tell that such a pretty girl could have so much efficiency." His misconception of women is largely responsible for Mary's success in completely dominating him, for she carefully cloaks her aggressive manipulation in feminine frailty.

For her part, Mary is dedicated to the impossible task of creating something perfect, a beautiful reflection of herself which will remain forever unchanged. As the workmen finish landscaping, she says to her husband: "We won't ever change it, will we, Harry? If a bush dies, we'll put another one just like it in the same place. . . . If anything should be changed it would be like part of me being torn out." But neither the garden nor Mary's life can be completely perfect, because there are always dangers in the world waiting to destroy the beautiful. The threat to the garden comes from the wild foliage of the ill which would destroy its order and serenity were it not for the sturdy but exotic line of fuschias, "little symbolic trees," obviously representing Mary. The hill too is a symbol—a symbol for everything that is not Mary. It, like Harry, opposes the irrationality of feeling and happenstance to her unemotional rationality.

Ironically perhaps, Mary's love for the garden does not imply a love of nature, for she reacts violently against the natural biological order which would alter her arrangement. Harry is appointed killer of the pests that come in the night to attack her garden, but, though he does not see it, she is the one who most relishes the slaughter:

> Mary held the flashlight while Harry did the actual killing, crushing the slugs and snails into oozy, bubbling masses. He knew it must be a disgusting business to her, but the light never wavered. "Brave girl," he thought. "She has a sturdiness in back of that fragile beauty." She made the hunts exciting too. "There's a big one, creeping and creeping," she would say. "He's after that big bloom. Kill him! Kill him quickly!" They came into the house after the hunts laughing happily.

Harry, however, declines to kill other animals for her sake. Although he meekly accepts her absolute refusal to allow him to own a dog which might "do things on the plants in her garden, or even dig in her flower beds," he will not set out poison for the cat which had crept from the hill into her garden and was threatening the birds. He argues that "animals suffer terribly when they get poison," and despite Mary's indifference to that argument, he insists that an air rifle will work as an effective deterrent once the cat has been stung by a pellet. Harry may realize subconsciously that the cat is symbolic of him just as the white quail is of Mary. It is evident that Mary, at least, sees the cat as a threat to her: "That white quail was *me*, the secret me that no one can ever get at, the me that's way inside. . . . Can't you see, dear? The cat was after me. It was going to kill me. That's why I want to poison it."

—Marilyn L. Mitchell, "Steinbeck's Strong Women: Feminist Identity in the Short Stories" in *Steinbeck's Women: Essays in Criticism*, ed. Tetsumaro Hayashi (Muncie, Ind.: The Steinbeck Society of America, 1979): pp. 28–30.

STANLEY RENNER ON SYMBOLISM IN "THE WHITE QUAIL"

[Stanley Renner is associate professor of English at Illinois State University, Normal, Illinois. In this excerpt he shows how the symbolic predatory cat and white quail dramatize the story's mounting friction between husband and wife, providing evidence for the detrimental effects of the Victorian "idealization of woman":]

With great figurative indirection the story suggests the growing tension in the Tellers' relationship. Mary gives herself with increasing ardor to her dream of inviolable purity, ultimately achieving a sense of disembodiment, of being pure spirit—"only essence, only mind and sight." Meanwhile, she senses an increasing threat to her idealized selfhood in the incipient rebellion of her husband, who refuses to put out poison for any cats that might threaten the birds in the garden. This growing tension, a symbolic representation of Harry's increasing sexual frustration and Mary's increasing determination to secure herself against it by withdrawing still further out of reach into the sanctuary of the ideal, culminates in the appearance in Mary's garden of the white quail and the cat that stalks it. With what is almost an orgasmic thrill, Mary recognizes the white quail as the perfected idealization of herself, "like the essence of me, an essence boiled down to utter purity." However, Mary's rapturous identification of the white quail with "everything beautiful" is ironically undercut by Harry's unwitting implication that it is something of a freak, a bloodless grotesquerie, "an albino. No pigment in the feathers, or something like that." The cat, obviously, is Harry, or, rather the irrepressible feral sexual urge deep in his unconscious mind and thus beyond his conscious control that stalks his wife despite his idealistic effort to drive it away.

In Mary's hysterical reaction to the threat of the cat, which we may take as an oblique representation of her response to the actual sexual advances of her husband, the story anatomizes the sexual revulsion and fear that have traditionally been associated with the idealized woman. Sexual matters were "things Mary didn't like to talk about": at Harry's timid confession of hunger for her "a little expression of annoyance crossed her face." Repelled by the approach of the cat, symbolizing her husband's sexuality, "she shuddered when he touched her." Thus Mary, who has declared, "I don't want any animals in my garden, any kind," rejects natural sexuality as threatening and vile. "Nature," Simpson observes, "is the enemy." Mary "reacts violently," Mitchell agrees, "against the natural biological order which would alter her arrangement." Mary's problem is not, however, merely a case of the spiritualized elevation of love above the coupling of animals nor even the Victorian revulsion at the vileness of male lust. It is a case of fear. Her hysteria stems from an association of sexual intercourse with a fearful tearing of her body and death. Any threat to the inviolability of her garden, Mary warns, would be "like part of me being torn out." Her terrible imagined vision of sexual defloration, even by her husband, is implied, with masterful understatement, in the undescribed but subtly implied picture of the cat tearing the white quail. Probing deeply into the roots of female sexual reticence, Steinbeck suggests that Mary associates the violation of her intactness with the destruction of her selfhood, her individuality. Thus she says, "The cat [figuratively Harry's sexual hunger] was after me—the secret me that no one can ever get at, the me that's way inside." The story seems to support a hypothesis for which a good deal of general evidence could be assembled that whereas the male tends to associate sexuality with life (*vide* "To His Coy Mistress"), the female is more susceptible to fears of depletion, diminution, destruction of selfhood, even death: the "gray cat" and the sexual threat it symbolizes "crept like death out of the brush," and Mary cries, "growing hysterical again, . . . 'it was going to kill me.'"

—Stanley Renner, "Sexual Idealism and Violence in 'The White Quail'," *Steinbeck Quarterly* 17, no. 3/4 (Summer-Fall 1984): pp. 83–84.

STANLEY RENNER ON MARY TELLER AND
SUE BRIDEHEAD

[In this excerpt, Stanley Renner discusses similarities between Thomas Hardy's Sue Bridehead (in *Jude the Obscure*) and Mary Teller, both of whom cause their men to feel revulsion towards natural sexuality and, ultimately, themselves:]

The dramatic conflict in both stories develops from the incompatability between the spiritualization of love and the natural sexual instincts of the male. Despite their earnest complicity in the idealism of the women, both Jude and Harry are unable to stifle their carnal desires. Both feel guilty for their vile weakness, but in Harry the conflict remains unconscious, while Jude accuses himself openly. "It seemed to make [Harry] ashamed when he turned the knob and found the door locked" to Mary's bedroom, but he never admits his inner turmoil into consciousness. Jude, however, considers himself "a wicked worthless fellow" among "poor unfortunate wretches of grosser substance," because of his irrepressible "animal passion." But since neither is able to purify himself from sexuality, both suffer classic cases of sexual frustration. Again, Jude agonizes openly, complaining to Sue about her unresponsiveness. The only sign of the unconscious revolt growing within Harry is his refusal to poison the cat, a growing threat to the birds in the garden.

But all parties suffer in such relationships—the women pressed to violate their delicate sensibilities as well as their bodies, the men tormented by desires which they themselves despise but can neither suppress nor satisfy. To some extent we may speculate that Hardy and Steinbeck may be telling their own stories: both, when they wrote these works, were in marriages troubled by incompatibility. But mainly they tell a larger story of the trouble in marriage caused by the spiritualization of love. Viewing human beings as creatures of nature, Hardy and Steinbeck attack the willful ignorance and over-refined refusal, by women particularly, of "natural forces"—the biological realities underlying the conjugal relationship. Jude comes to understand that Sue "does not realize what marriage means," and Hardy explains her unconcern for the torment she causes men in the nonsexual intimacies she cultivates as childish ignorance "of that side of their natures which wore out women's hearts and lives." As Mary plans the garden that represents the spiritual marriage she desires, she ignores the needs of the male involved, thinking not "'Would this man like such a garden?' but, 'Would the garden like such a man?'"

Thus Hardy and Steinbeck portray a state of marriage in which "the normal sex impulses are turned into devilish domestic gins" that torment the hapless creatures of nature trapped in them. Since, however, the relationships in *Jude the Obscure* and "The White Quail" are established on women's terms to suit their own sexual aversion, they are a particularly bad bargain for men. Jude complains of having "danced attendance on [Sue] so long for such poor returns": "You concede nothing to me," he tells her, "and I have to concede everything to you." Steinbeck makes the same point figuratively in the Tellers' conversation about Harry's job in a loan company, which ironically underscores Mary's refusal of her end of the traditional marriage bargain. Making exceedingly "poor returns" herself on Harry's investment in her comfortable domestic arrangements, Mary questions the fairness of the loan agreements that provide Harry's livelihood. But it is her own willful, self-serving blindness and unfairness that is exposed in her notion that "it would do [Harry] no harm to see what business really was like." Doubly ironic is her acknowledgment that "every one has a right to make a living," when, only six lines later, Harry is turned away yet again from her locked bedroom door.

> —Stanley Renner, "Mary Teller and Sue Bridehead: Birds of a Feather in 'The White Quail' and *Jude the Obscure*," *Steinbeck Quarterly* 18, no. 1/2 (Winter/Spring 1985): pp. 42–44.

ROBERT S. HUGHES ON THE STORY AS AUTOBIOGRAPHY AND ITS THEMES

[Robert S. Hughes, who teaches at the University of Hawaii at Manoa, has written *Beyond the Red Pony* (1987) and *John Steinbeck: A Study of the Short Fiction* (1988). In this excerpt, he suggests reading the story biographically, in which both loneliness and the desire for immutability are crucial themes:]

The biographical nature of "The White Quail" may explain what Stanley Young calls its "unusual emotional province." A reflection of Steinbeck's life during this time, the narrative can be seen as a study of a failing marriage, which focuses first on the wife's fixation and aloofness from her husband and then on the husband's consequent loneliness and resentment. Brian Barbour points out that such a shift in focus (from Mary to Harry Teller) diminishes the story's emotional power, for what begins as an expose of Mary's diseased imagination, culminates in a flash of violence when Harry kills the symbol of his wife's changeless purity—the white quail. The story ends without resolution. Harry, as a result of shooting the quail, feels remorse and increased loneliness. Mary remains unchanged.

Over the years, critics have suggested other themes for "The White Quail." The most unusual of them is Arthur L. Simpson's contention that Mary Teller constitutes Steinbeck's "Portrait of an Artist" (i.e., she is obsessed with her artistic creation [garden] to the exclusion of human warmth and compassion). Other critics have seen the story as a chronicle of a narcissist, the tale of a Platonic idealist, and a symbolic representation of sexual tension exploding into violence. But the themes of loneliness and fear of change are particularly central, since each can be identified with one of the two characters, and both feelings are evidenced in the life of the author at this time.

The story's setting, like Mary Teller's garden, is unusually static. The scene never shifts from the Teller home and yard. The story unfolds in six numbered sections, each indicating a change in time. Between sections one (Harry's proposal) and two (landscaping of the garden), the longest stretch of time elapses. Except when a cat threatens the white quail in section one and when Harry shoots the quail in section six, the story has little overt action. In addition to giving the story a generally static setting, Steinbeck omits details about the physical appearance of the characters. The reader may not notice this omission, though, since Mary's psyche is so thoroughly linked with her garden, and her "essence" with the white quail. Harry, on the other hand, is identified with the "grey cat" preying on Mary's quail. He not only refuses to poison the cat, but also kills the symbolic bird. Antoni Gajewski equates Harry with such other "enemies" as snails, dogs, and common garden pests that plague Mary.

The story's principal strength is neither its plot nor its characters. Its distinctive quality can more accurately be called "lyric." Like a lyric poem, "The White Quail" is primarily an expression of the writer's emotions—loneliness and fear of change, as we have seen. But, below the level of the author's consciousness, more sinister meanings surely lurk. The white quail represents beauty, purity, and helplessness, and is the crowning glory of Mary's private, ordered, and timeless garden. The cat is a predator, a threat to the symbol of Mary's inner self. Whether Harry realizes it or not, he has an affinity with the cat. And whether he wills it or not, he shoots quail, not cat.

—Robert S. Hughes, *Beyond the Red Pony: A Reader's Companion to Steinbeck's Complete Short Stories* (Metuchen, N.J.: The Scarecrow Press Inc., 1987): pp. 63–64.

JOHN H. TIMMERMAN ON MARY TELLER AND THE ROMANTIC IMAGINATION

[John H. Timmerman teaches at Calvin College, Grand Rapids, Michigan, and is author of *John Steinbeck's Fiction: The Aesthetics of the Road Taken* (1986) and *The Dramatic Landscape of Steinbeck's Short Fiction* (1990). This selection suggests brilliant connections between Mary Teller's worship of the imagination and Romantic articulations from Milton to Blake and Browning:]

Like some of the Romantic Movement poets of the preceding century, Mary Teller deifies the imagination, often at the expense of reality. Speaking of Blake and Coleridge in *The Romantic Imagination*, C. M. Bowra observes, "They reject [Locke's] conception of the universe, and replace it by their own systems, which deserve the name of 'idealist' because mind is their central point and governing factor. But because they are poets, they insist that the most vital activity of the mind is the imagination. Since for them it is the very source of spiritual energy, they cannot but believe that it is divine, and that, when they exercise it, they in some way partake of the activity of God."

In much the same way, Mary Teller has become her own divinity, and her garden has become a sacred manifestation of that divine mind. Bowra states, "For Blake the imagination is nothing less than God as He operates in the human soul. It follows that any act of creation formed by the imagination is divine and that in the imagination man's spritual nature is fully and finally realized." Having made one's own kingdom by the divine power of the imagination, the huge danger, for both the Romantics and Mary Teller, is the expurgation from that garden of all reality. Reality represents the defilement of Eden, the serpent from the wilds.

"The White Quail" thereby takes its place very much in the lineage of a number of literary gardens. From Spenser to the modern age, the garden represents an unspoiled order, but also an artificial order severed from life. The garden, after the Genesis fall, is disordered, and humans must make the best of their way in it. In Milton's *Paradise Lost,* Michael admonishes Eve,

> Lament not, Eve, but patiently resign
> What justly thou hast lost; nor set thy heart,
> Thus over-fond, on that which is not thine;
> Thy going is not lonely, with thee goes
> Thy husband, him to follow thou art bound;
> Where he abides, think there thy native soil.

The words might well have been directed to Mary Teller, for her clinging to the artifice of her garden divorces her from the companionship of her husband. Her "native soil" is forsaken for the ethereal soil of the romantic garden.

In the same way, Steinbeck found that an artwork which divorces itself from life, which finds life threatening and abhorrent, is despicable. Mary Teller's garden is a bit like Andrea del Sarto's paintings in Robert Browning's poem; yet, Mary lacks del Sarto's understanding: "All is silver-grey / Placid and perfect with my art: the worse!" While del Sarto laments the fact, Mary clings to it as an ultimate reality. In his analysis of Browning's poetry, Roma King observes, "Art significantly is not an analogy for or a symbol of the Infinite. Neither is it a platform from which man leaps from this world into another. On the contrary, art fixes firmly on this world, circumscribing man's activities, indeed, but at the same time imbuing his finite efforts with a boundless significance." Mary Teller's garden is the opposite of the one King describes, or that del Sarto wishes he could reach, for it is a sterile world of imaginary symbols eternally separated from life. Of this garden Stanley Renner comments, "Steinbeck has deftly symbolized the romantic ideal that lies at the heart of it all, a spiritualized, sexless, and thus, in several senses, pointless love."

—John H. Timmerman, *The Dramatic Landscape of Steinbeck's Short Stories* (Norman, Okla.: University of Oklahoma Press, 1990): pp. 180–81.

CHRISTOPHER S. BUSCH ON THE STORY'S DEPICTION OF FAILED AGRARIANISM

[Christopher S. Busch is assistant professor of English at Hillsdale College, Hillsdale, Michigan. In this excerpt he analyzes the story as a frontier narrative in which Mary Teller is a debased yeoman and her husband a similarly diminished hunter:]

In "The White Quail" Steinbeck describes the protagonist, Mary Teller, as a diminished modern yeoman who attempts to create a perfect garden in the post-frontier West. Mary's husband, Harry, contributes to this project for a time, but ultimately recognizes its perverse nature and hunts down and kills the white quail, which, in Mary's mind, symbolizes the garden's perfection. Owens argues that "Mary's garden is an attempt to construct an unfallen Eden in a fallen world, a neurotic projection of Mary's self." He concludes that the story ultimately reveals "the futility of holding to the Eden myth—even the danger of the illusion." In describing Mary as yeoman and Harry as hunter, however, Steinbeck does not sharply undercut the myth of agrarianism as Owens suggests. Intead, by revealing the degenerate nature of the characters' personalities and actions, Steinbeck satirizes the narcissism and pathological self-delusion that cripple the modern American imagination and reflect the culture's degeneration.

As a frontier-based narrative, Steinbeck's story achieves much of its power through the dualistic quality of its setting and characters. Steinbeck purposely sets the story on a "frontier," or borderland possessing attributes of both a wilderness and a Crèvecoeurian "middle region" to emphasize the story's thematic connection with frontier history:

> Right at the edge of the garden, the hills started up, wild with cascara bushes and poison oak, with dry grass and live oak, very wild. If you didn't go around to the front of the house, you couldn't tell it was on the very edge of town.

This setting functions as a modern suburban frontier, similar in appearance to the historical frontier, but diminished in size, a kind of mock frontier. The setting is both like the historical frontier and unlike it at the same time, just as the characters are both types and antitypes of mythic frontier figures.

In her effort to tame this frontier and transform it into a garden, Mary Teller appears to be a descendent of the homesteader, or yeoman, celebrated in agrarian myth. Yet, in actuality, Mary is a diminished yeoman whose approach to nature inverts the yeoman's traditional approach to the land. Where the pioneer yeoman saw opportunity in the wilderness and approached it with expectancy, Mary sees danger in "the dark thickets of the hill": "'That's the enemy,' Mary said one time. 'That's the world that wants to get in, all rough and tangled and unkempt.'" Where the yeoman gained strength and virtue through contact with the soil, Mary protects herself from contact with nature by wearing a "sunbonnet" and "good sturdy gloves," and hires workers to carry out the actual labor.

Harry joins his wife on this suburban frontier as a diminished hunter, reminiscent of the Wild West hunter in the Leatherstocking tradition, yet curiously distinct from that type as well. Like the hunter, Harry appears near the story's end as a skilled marksman more at home in the wilderness of the hill beyond the garden than in the garden itself. But in his unconsidered acquiescence to Mary's neurotic wishes, his choice of an air gun as a weapon, and his pursuit of the harmless white quail as prey, Harry becomes a ridiculous figure, scarcely resembling the self-reliant frontier hunter whose "physical strength, adaptability to nature, resourcefulness and courage" defined him as a heroic type.

—Christopher S. Busch, "Longing for the Lost Frontier: Steinbeck's Vision of Cultural Decline in 'The White Quail' and 'The Chrysanthemums,'" in *Steinbeck Quarterly* 22, no. 1/2 (Winter-Spring 1989): pp. 83–84.

CHARLOTTE HADELLA ON HARRY'S DELIBERATE KILLING OF THE WHITE QUAIL

[Charlotte Hadella teaches English at Arkansas State University and has published articles on Steinbeck and William Gass. The excerpt below argues, contra Renner, that Harry's killing of the white quail is intentional:]

Part III of the story features the description of the couple killing slugs and snails together in the garden, the introduction of the threatening cat, and Mary's speech proclaiming her fuschias as a fortress from the "rough and tangled" world that wants to get into her garden. Critics agree that Harry's sexual needs are identified with the stalking cat which is mentioned in Part III, preparing the reader for the information in Part IV that Mary always locked her bedroom door and that "Harry always tried the door silently." Mary muses that it "seemed to make him ashamed when he turned the knob and found the door locked," but her response is to turn out the light in her bedroom and look out the window "at her garden in the half moonlight." In this way Steinbeck shows Mary retreating farther into her unnatural world of illusory perception as Harry becomes less able to suppress his natural sexual urges.

Though Renner is correct in noting that the final two sections of the story "move toward a striking climax that dramatizes the potential of the unconscious stresses building up in the marriage," his contentions that Harry kills the quail unintentionally, and that this act shows Harry finally succumbing to his sexual urges in spite of Mary's protests, seem contradictory. It is more logical to assume that in a world as symbolically contrived as the world of the Tellers' marriage, Steinbeck allows Harry to kill the white quail intentionally. Harry's violence against the symbol of Mary's chastity, "an essence boiled down to utter purity," is a symbolic action by a character who is incapable of real action. It is also important to note that the cat does not even enter into the picture in this scene. Mary's hysterical reaction may have scared him away from her garden forever; or Harry may have simply *become* the cat, symbolically.

Steinbeck includes a subtle detail in Part V of the story to under-line Mary's ability to dominate Harry so thoroughly that he is only capable of symbolic violence. Just after she sees the white quail, Mary experiences a series of memories that she associates with the kind of pleasure she feels at that moment. One of those memories is simply a statement someone once made about her—"She's like a gentian, so quiet"—a statement which filled her with "an ecstasy" like the ecstasy in seeing that white quail. A gentian is a medicinal plant that destroys bacteria, and Mary, like a gentian, has sterilized her marriage completely, so completely that Harry is incapable of contaminating it even if he refuses to poison the cat.

—Charlotte Hadella, "Steinbeck's Cloistered Women" in *The Steinbeck Question*, ed. Donald Noble (Troy, N.Y.: Whitson Publishers, 1993): pp. 67–68.

Plot Summary of
"Flight"

In "Flight," we are introduced to Mexican-American family life in Monterey County, California. Mama Torres and her three children—Pepé, Emilio, and Rosy—live on a crumbling farm where they struggle for survival. Mama's husband died a decade before from a rattlesnake bite on his chest. Widowhood causes her to rely on sparse livestock and the fishing skills of her black children, Emilio and Rosy, ages twelve and fourteen. When it is safe to do so, she keeps them from school so that they can fish for her.

The story revolves around her 19-year-old son Pepé, whose Indian features and slothfulness separate him from his admiring siblings. Emilio and Rosy enjoy watching him play with his prized possession, a knife from his father, as he flicks it onto a redwood post fifteen feet in front of him. His mother chides him for his inactivity, and tells him she has a task for him: to ride the horse into town and get medicine. She also tells him to say prayers at church, visit a friend, Mrs. Rodriguez, for overnight accommodations, and to buy some sweets for the children. Pepé is grateful and excited by the newly acquired responsibility and asks to wear his father's green handkerchief and hatband for the journey. He assures her that he is a "man" now, but she calls him "toy-baby," "big lazy," and "a peanut." As he confidently rides off, Mama tells the young children that Pepé is almost a man and that he will become one when a man is needed.

Late that night Pepé returns home earlier than expected, since he was expected to stay with the family friend, Mrs. Rodriguez. He tells Mama he had wine at the Rodriguez house and that he must go away. She sees that an important change has taken place in him because his soft facial features have hardened and his playfulness has turned to glumness. Finally, he blurts out that he has killed a man who insulted his father and that he must run away. She quickly packs for him his father's gun, some jerky, a water bag, and awakes the children to bid him farewell. She instructs him not to sleep even when tired, to pray, and to beware the mysterious "dark watchers." He declares, "I am a man," and then leaves. After he departs, she bravely starts the traditional death wail, believing her son never will return, and the children discuss their brother's transition into manhood. Emilio asks if he has really died, and Rosy wisely answers, "not yet."

The rest of the story concerns Pepé's solitary journey in the Californian wilderness as he tries to escape his pursuers. Throughout, the story's point of view is extremely sympathetic to his plight. On his first day, he finds an established path in the morning sun and stays on it through a canyon, passing waterfalls and green foliage. Although the redwoods soon block the sky, ample signs of lushness and life permeate the atmosphere, like berries by the stream, leafy trees, and moss.

Soon, however, the vegetation gives way to aridity: lizards and broken rock appear, a bird ominously "creaks," and the previous greenness turns into into bare rock. When a dark stranger appears to be watching him, Pepé looks away. Tired, he keeps riding, navigating the difficult path and struggling with the hot, dry air. A "dark watcher" momentarily appears above him on a cliff. A harmless wildcat crosses his path, and he sleeps when the moon rises.

Near dawn Pepé awakes at the sound of his horse and another one whinnying. He gets onto the trail as light comes. His horse is suddenly shot dead and Pepé hides behind a bush, trying to escape his unseen assailant. His movements become snakelike, as he ducks behind granite, slinks on the ground, and points his rifle defensively in all directions. After looking around, he fires a shot down the trail. The answering shot sends a piece of granite through his hand between the knuckles. He stops the bleeding with a spider's web but must transfer the rifle to his left hand. His mouth swells with thirst, and he is reduced to a difficult crawl because his hand causes great pain. As night falls the hand pounds harder and his tongue fills his mouth; he still has no water. He travels in the moonlight until no soil but only rock surrounds him. When finally he arrives at a stream's bed at the bottom of a hill, no water awaits him; his head falls into the muddy earth and he sleeps.

In the late afternoon he awakens to discover a mountain lion staring at him, but like the wildcat, the lion lets him be. In the evening Pepé hears a horse and dog in the distance, braces himself for a confrontation, but falls asleep again from exhaustion. When he rises, he cannot find his gun and his arm is swollen with gangrene.

Instead of forming words he can only hiss. When morning comes, he lets pus out of the wound, exacerbating the pain but taking his mind off his situation. By this point his tongue is black, his arm causes him great agony, and he once again hears the dogs. Pepé crosses himself and stands on a peak. He is shot multiple times. His body collapses and rolls down the hill, an avalanche taking shape with him and covering his head.

During Pepé's lonely flight through the wilderness, the landscape transforms from wet and nourishing to dry and deadly. As he travels, his movements get slower, and his body weakens. Pepé also loses his goods as the story progresses: he loses his hat just before his horse is shot; after his hand is wounded, he sheds his father's coat, and, finally, the evening before his death he leaves his rifle and his knife behind. He loses the ability to speak towards the end, reduced to the hiss of a snake. However, he does stand up to confront his fate—final justice. ❀

List of Characters in
"Flight"

At the story's beginning, *Pepé Torres* is considered a lazy but adorable boy of nineteen. He is tall, with long, loose limbs, straight black hair, chiseled cheekbones and chin, and a feminine mouth. He does not seem to have a strong sense of responsibility, spending his time flicking his knife, a gift of his deceased father, into a redwood post, to the squeals of delight coming from his two younger siblings. When his Mama sends him into town on an errand, with great vanity he asks to wear his father's hatband and green handkerchief, assuring his mother of his manliness. He returns early from that errand, having become a "man" (according to himself) because he killed another man who insulted his father. He appears less funloving and much more serious. At this juncture Pepé is forced to flee into the forest and later into the desert where many threats increasingly challenge his survival: "dark watchers," unseen but heard assailants, an injured hand turned gangrenous, and lack of food and water. In awful succession he loses his horse, hat, coat, rifle, knife, and his ability to speak.

While *Mama Torres* only appears in the story's opening pages, she seems to be a commanding figure in the lives of her children. A widow, Mama Torres manages her farm and supervises her two younger children, who sometimes catch fish to feed the family. She dotes on her eldest child, Pepé, and prides herself on raising him up to support the family. After he leaves because he has killed a man, she mourns, knowing she will never see him again. ❁

Critical Views on
"Flight"

PETER LISCA ON THE STORY'S CONTRADICTORY
MORAL MESSAGES

[Peter Lisca has written *The Wide World of John Steinbeck*
(1958) and *John Steinbeck: Nature and Myth* (1978). In this
excerpt from *The Wide World of John Steinbeck*, Lisca discusses the story's two competing messages: humankind
tends toward our "baser," animalistic instincts, and yet
affirms what separates us from beasts. He is also struck by
the theatricality of the story's ending:]

The flight itself has meaning on two planes. On the physical level,
Pepé's penetration into the desert mountains is directly proportional
to his increasing separation from civilized man and his reduction to
the state of wild animal. The extent to which this process has gone is
measured by his encounters with a wildcat and later a mountain
lion, both of whom regard Pepé with a calm curiosity, not yet having
learned to fear man. The symbolic meaning of Pepé's flight moves in
the opposite direction. On this level, the whole action of the story
goes to show man, even when stripped of all his civilized accoutrements (like Ahab of his pipe, sextant, and hat), is still something
more than an animal. This is the purpose of Pepé's losing consecu-
tively his horse (escape), his hat (protection from nature), and his
gun (physical defense), to face his inevitable death not with the
headlong retreat or futile death struggle of an animal, but with the
calm and stoicism required by the highest conception of manhood,
forcing fate to give him a voice in the "how" if not the "what" of his
destiny. It is worth remarking that perhaps Steinbeck achieves this
significant symbolic meaning of the story's ending at some expense
of verisimilitude. The boy standing exposed on the high rock and
taking his death is "theatrical" in the same way that the ending of
almost every one of Steinbeck's novels is "theatrical"—not incredible
or contrived so much as disjunctive, incongruous in realistic terms
because of its too perfect symbolic congruity. This type of ending is
one of Steinbeck's most consistent stylistic devices, and his persistent
use of it in the face of almost unanimous adverse criticism must
indicate that for him, at least, the important action to be terminated

in his novels exists not on the physical plane, but on the symbolic. When these endings are examined in light of the whole work, it becomes evident that their incongruity with the surface "realism" is overshadowed by their bringing into sharper focus the substrata of symbolism and allegory.

—Peter Lisca, *The Wide World of John Steinbeck* (New Brunswick, N.J.: Rutgers University Press, 1958): pp. 99–100.

PETER LISCA ON INITIATION RITUALS IN "FLIGHT"

[In this extract from *John Steinbeck: Nature and Myth* (1978), Peter Lisca notes that the story lacks a life-giving initiation ritual through which Pepé could enter manhood:]

"Flight," among the best of the short stories in *The Long Valley*, is, on one level, a simple one. A boy unthinkingly kills a man, takes flight, is pursued, and is himself deliberately killed. The writing is Steinbeck at his best—poetic in its rhythm and images, yet terse and realistic. On another level, however, it is a story of initiation, or perhaps *lack* of it. Most of the story concerns details of the boy Pepé's flight into the desolate granite mountains, where he finds that there is no escaping the consequences of having asserted his manhood—by resenting an insult and throwing his knife into a stranger as unerringly as earlier that same day he had playfully thrown it into a post. In his flight, he gradually loses his horse, his hat, and his gun, which are the heritage from his father and the trappings of civilization. So that at the end, entirely alone, escape hopeless and his right arm swelling with infection, he stands up in full view to take his pursuer's death shot with a dignity and purposeful courage that demonstrate he has found the true test of manhood in his death. Possibly, Pepé's failure to survive the advent of his manhood is related to the fact that he had not known his father and grew up in isolation with his mother and her younger children. He does not undergo a ritual preparation under the careful tutelage of an adult male, a sponsor; rather, with no preparation he is thrown from boyhood directly into an adult situation. Thus, unlike Root, Jim, and Tom, he does not undergo a rebirth, but rather returns entirely to the earth, which in the story's last sentence buries him in a little avalanche of broken rocks.

—Peter Lisca, *John Steinbeck: Nature and Myth* (Toronto: Fitzhenry & Whiteside Ltd., 1978): p. 194–95.

Dan Vogel on Watching Pepe's Transition to Adulthood

[Dan Vogel was dean and associate professor at Stern College, Yeshiva University in New York City during the early 1960s. He is author of *Emma Lazarus* (1980) and *The Three Masks of American Tragedy* (1974). In the following paragraphs he considers the story a myth that explains the ritual of experiencing adulthood; unlike Lisca, he maintains that the transition from boyhood to manhood occurs, despite its fatal consequences:]

The ordeal of transformation from innocence to experience, from purity to defilement begins. There is the physical pain of the ordeal, symbolized by a cut hand that soon becomes gangrenous. There is the psychological pain: the recognition of a strangeness in life that is omnipresent, silent, watchful, and dark—the sense of Evil, or Tragedy, or Retribution. The realization is symbolized by the narratively gratuitous, unrealistic presence of the black figures, the "dark watchers" who are seen for a moment on the tops of the ridges and then disappear. "No one knew who the watchers were," Steinbeck tells us, "nor where they lived, but it was better to ignore them and never to show interest in them. They did not bother one who stayed on the trail and minded his own business." They are not the posse, who are physical figures behind Pepé with horses and guns and dogs. These are the silent inscrutable watchers from above, the universal Nemesis, the recognition of which signals a further step into manhood.

Pepé meets wild animals face to face, but they are quiescent and harmless. They seem to recognize a fellow creature who also lives for a moment in a wilderness, they in the throes of an instinctive existence, he in the playing out of an inevitable phenomenon. He is no danger to them.

Clambering over rocks, staggering across sunbaked flats, fleeing before sounds and shapes, Pepé forgets his father's hat; his father's horse is shot out from under him, and his father's saddle is now useless. He divests himself of his father's coat because it pains his swollen, gangrenous arm, and in his pain he leaves his father's rifle on the trail behind him.

Only now, having been separated from his mother and having cleansed himself of all the accoutrements and artifacts of his father, can the youth stand alone. But to Steinbeck this is far from a joyous or victorious occasion. It is sad and painful and tragic. Pepé rises to his feet, "black against the morning sky," astride a ridge. He is a perfect target and the narrative ends with the man against the sky shot down. The body rolls down the hillside, creating a little avalanche, which follows him in his descent and covers up his head. Thus innocence is killed and buried in the moment that Man stands alone.

Thus the myth ends, as so many myths do, with violence and melodrama. What the myth described is the natural miracle of entering manhood. When serenity of childhood is lost, there is pain and misery, but there is nevertheless a sense of gain and heroism which are more interesting and dramatic. It is a story that has fascinated many from Wordsworth to Hemingway, and what Steinbeck has written is a myth that describes in symbols what has happened to each of us.

—Dan Vogel, "Steinbeck's 'Flight': The Myth of Manhood," *College English* 23, no. 3 (December 1961): p. 226.

JOHN ANTICO ON CHRISTIAN TRIADS IN THE STORY

[John Antico taught English at Michigan's Lansing Community College in the mid-1960s. His Ph.D. is from Wayne State University. He has published fiction and his research subjects have included J. D. Salinger and Edward Albee. Below he provides ample evidence for the story's Christian dimension in the frequently used motif of triads:]

If one is determined to find triads in almost any story, it is not difficult to "force" them out of the text, but in "Flight" there are numerous triads of such significance that in the context of the religious overtones already mentioned, they beome meaningful aspects of Steinbeck's main theme. It has been noted that the story is divided into three distinct sections: (1) Pepé's errand to Monterey, (2) his return and departure, and (3) his flight through the mountains. Pepé's flight covers a span of three days and three nights. He ascends three ridges and descends into and crosses two valleys, noting the next one from the top of the third ridge: "Below him lay a deep canyon exactly like the last, waterless and desolate." There are three watering places, there are three dark watchers, and Pepé's knife is used three times. In almost all of these triads, particularly the last three, the third one is significantly different from the first two. The knife is used in play the first two times: "Pepé's wrist flicked like the head of a snake. The blade seemed to fly open in mid air . . . " The third time it is used is when it kills the man in Monterey: ". . . it went almost by itself. It flew, it darted before Pepé knew it." The first two watering places are regular watering places—the stream and the well, where Pepé waters the horse as well as filling his water bag— while the third is a collection of muddy water at the bottom of the hole Pepé digs in the ground, where Pepé "waters" himself in much the same way an animal might. As for the dark watchers, Pepé sees two of them, on the top of the ridges ahead, but the third dark watcher is Pepé himself on top of the third ridge. Furthermore, although he does not voluntarily descend toward the third valley, when is killed, "his body jarred back," and he rolls down the slope toward the third valley. There are other triads of minor importance, but one final one worth noting is the three specific references made to the direction of Pepé's flight. The light imagery in all three is significant: (1) "Against the *east* the piling mountains were misty with light"; (2) "*Eastward* the bare rock mountaintops were pale and powder-dry under the dropping sun"; and (3) "The bright evening light washed the *eastern* ridge." The first reference occurs at the beginning of the second section of the story, and the light is from the morning sun; the last two occur in the third section and refer to the evening sun. The direction of Pepé's flight from civilization is appropriately eastward toward the cradle of western civilization.

—John Antico, "A Reading of Steinbeck's 'Flight'," *Modern Fiction Studies* 11, no. 1 (Spring 1965): pp. 52–53. ☙

[Mimi Gladstein received her Ph.D. from the University of New Mexico, teaches at the University of Texas in El Paso where she is interim director of Women's Studies, and publishes in *College English*, *Steinbeck Quarterly*, and *Rocky Mountain Review*. She has also written *The Ayn Rand Companion* (1984) and *The Indestructible Woman in Faulkner, Hemingway and Steinbeck* (1986). In this excerpt from an article on Steinbeck's female characters, she refreshingly concentrates on a much-neglected character in the story, Mama Torres:]

Perhaps the best example of an indestructible woman in a short story is Mama Torres in "Flight." Mama Torres has suffered much. She struggles to eke a meager living from a barren land and stingy sea. She is described as "a lean, dry woman with ancient eyes." She had been the sole support of her family ever since the day, ten years earlier, when "her husband tripped over a stone and fell full length on a rattlesnake." Mama Torres is resigned to her hard lot. She accepts what comes. The big test of her ability to endure comes when her oldest child Pepé reaches manhood, or thinks he has. Mama Torres must allow her boy-child to become a man in his own right even though it is extremely painful for her. With the traditional patience of woman, she views his typically boyish pastime, throwing a knife. She has a woman's scorn for this aggressive action, but she is aware of its significance in his maturation: "Yes, thou art a man, my poor little Pepé; thou art a man. I have seen it coming on thee, I have watched you throwing the knife into the post, and I have been afraid."

Inevitably this prelude to aggressive masculine behavior leads to Pepé's killing a man. A man challenges him and he responds with a phallic symbol, the knife.

Pepé's aggression and knife-throwing identify him with manhood. But what manhood has to offer Pepé is being hunted down and killed. Mama Torres' nourishing behavior and endurance identify her with womanhood. Though her lot is pain, she endures. She summons the strength to send her first-born to an unknown destiny. First, however, she provides him with food, water, blankets, and a gun. She does what has to be done as she always has. Pepé looks for a crack in her invulnerability:

Pepé turned back to Mama. He seemed to look for a little softness, a little weakness in her. His eyes were searching, but Mama's face remained fierce. "Go now," she said. "Do not wait to be caught here like a chicken."

Mama Torres is strong enough not to break down in Pepé's presence. Only when he is gone does she break down and show her great unhappiness. Though Pepé is tracked down and killed, Mama Torres must endure to fulfill her woman's role. She remains with her other two children, undefeated and unbowed, mothering the new generation, male and female, symbolized by the two younger children in her family.

—Mimi Reisel Gladstein, "Female Characters in Steinbeck: Minor Characters of Major Importance?" in *Steinbeck's Women: Essays in Criticism*, ed. Tetsumaro Hayashi (Muncie, Ind.: The Steinbeck Society of America, 1979): pp. 22–23.

Edward J. Piacentino on Animal Imagery in the Story

[Edward J. Piacentino is associate professor of English at High Point College and writes on Twain, Faulkner, and Willa Cather, among others. Selections from his good, close analysis of animal imagery in the story attend to the story's openings paragraphs and the later stages of Pepé's flight:]

Animal imagery abounds in "Flight," from the reference in the first sentence to "hissing white waters" of the Pacific Ocean to the "thick hiss" that comes from Pepé's lips as he tries desperately to speak before he is shot and killed at the end. In characterizing Pepé near the outset, Steinbeck points out his "sharp Indian cheek bones" and his "eagle nose," the latter a suggestive image which serves to establish Pepé's primitive, animal-like nature. Mama Torres, Pepé's mother, likewise uses animal imagery in describing her son's laziness. As she tells Pepé, "Some lazy cow must have got into thy father's family, else how could I have a son like thee." And at an earlier time she tells Pepé, when she was pregnant with him, ". . . a sneaking lazy coyote came out of the brush and looked at me one day. That must have made thee so." The coyote mentioned here is, of course, a wild animal, an appropriate reference to highlight Pepé's primitive animalism. [...]

As Pepé progresses farther into the mountains, an environment of uncertainty and hostility, he seems to feel even more compelled to act in the manner of a hunted wild beast. When his horse is shot by one of the pursuers, Pepé, Steinbeck observes in the scene that follows, moves with the "instinctive care of an animal," "worming" and "wriggling" his way to safety behind a rock. The point Steinbeck seems to be making here is certainly not vague, for he emphasizes it throughout the story—namely, the naturalistic view that man must resort to behaving like a brute animal in his struggle to survive. Even though Pepé spots a single eagle flying overhead, free and unencumbered, just before his horse is shot, this eagle becomes ironic when viewed in retrospect and within the context of Pepé's own greatly restricted and reduced mobility, the result of the untimely loss of his horse and a painful, near maiming injury to his right hand.

Other animal references also serve a functional thematic purpose during the period of Pepé's flight. In fact, every successive animal image becomes more threatening and sinister than the ones that preceded it. Soon after the injury to his hand, Pepé views a number of wild animals in the following order of appearance: a small brown bird, a high-soaring eagle that "stepped daintily out on the trail and crossed it and disappeared into the brush again," a brown doe, a rattlesnake, grey lizards, a "big tawny mountain lion" that sits watching him, and last circling black birds, presumably buzzards, a universal portentous sign of disaster, in this case Pepé's own approaching death.

—Edward J. Piacentino, "Patterns of Animal Imagery in Steinbeck's 'Flight'," *Studies in Short Fiction* 17, no. 4 (Fall 1980): pp 438, 441.

JOHN H. TIMMERMAN ON THE ANIMALISTIC IMPULSE AND DARKNESS

[John Timmerman teaches at Calvin College, Grand Rapids, Michigan, and is author of *John Steinbeck's Fiction:*

The Aesthetics *of the Road Taken* (1986) and *The Dramatic Landscape of Steinbeck's Short Fiction* (1990). In this excerpt he incorporates other critical opinions to show how both debased, primitive instincts and the theme of darkness come to predominate in the story's development:]

In the hot, sun-blasted world of "Flight," however, when a lazy boy asserts his manhood with a knife, when civilization's code of conduct is violated and the posse mounts, man is very much reduced to an animal. One recalls Steinbeck's reflection in his notebook: "Oh man who in climbing up has become lower." Pepe's flight into the mountains is also a devolution, paced by a divestment of civilized tools and in incrementally intensifying animal imagery. He loses gun and knife, saddle, horse, and food. John Ditsky noted the pattern of loss: "Beyond the simple deterioration of his possessions—as when his clothing tears away or his flesh is ripped—leading to a contemplation of man's naked state like that in *King Lear,* there is the importance of the fact that the objects just named are Pepe's from his father; they are, as the knife is in fact described, 'his inheritance.' Pepe's attempt to sustain the manhood he has claimed in a single violent act—by means of tools which were his father's badge of manhood and his estate—fails; he is finally stripped down to what he brings with him within himself: his own gifts, his own courage."

Stripped of civilized tools, Pepe's movements are increasingly described in verbs that suggest a primordial or serpentine creature. Pepe "crawled," "wormed," "wriggled," "darted," flashed," "slid," "writhed," and "squirmed" in the final stages. Furthermore, his paralyzing thirst strips him of the one thing that separates humanity from animals—speech: "His tongue tried to make words, but only a thick hissing came from between his lips." Even his tongue becomes infected with blackness: "Between his lips the tip of his black tongue showed," and the only sound of which he is capable is a "thick hiss."

As several critics have mentioned, a third pattern is woven into the loss of civilized tools and the heavy use of animal imagery—the increasing images of darkness. From his early fascination with the lights on the altar and the sun-swept cliffs of his home, Pepe's world is subsumed by blackness, culminating in the dark watchers. He leaves for his flight on a morning when "moonlight and daylight fought with each other, and the two warring qualities made it difficult to see." Louis Owens observes:

The theme of death is woven on a thread of blackness through the story. It is Pepe's black knife which initiates the cycle of death. When Pepe flees he wears his dead father's black coat and black hat. It is the two "black ones," Rosy and Emilio, who prophesy Pepe's death. The line of gangrene running the length of Pepe's arm is black, foreshadowing his death, and it is the "dark watchers" who finally symbolize death itself. From the beginning of the story, Pepe grows increasingly dark, until in the end he will be black like the watchers.

The climactic final portrait is thick with darkness, and even as a new morning breaks the sky, the eagle, which has been present from the start, is replaced by predatory black vultures.

—John H. Timmerman, *The Dramatic Landscape of Steinbeck's Short Stories* (Norman, Okla.: University of Oklahoma Press, 1990): pp. 195–96.

Works by
John Steinbeck

Cup of Gold. 1929.

The Pastures of Heaven. 1932.

To a God Unknown. 1933.

Tortilla Flat. 1935.

In Dubious Battle. 1936.

Saint Katy the Virgin. 1936.

Nothing So Monstrous. 1936.

Of Mice and Men. 1937.

Of Mice and Men (drama). 1937.

The Red Pony. 1937.

The Long Valley. 1938.

Their Blood Is Strong. 1938.

The Grapes of Wrath. 1939.

John Steinbeck Replies. 1940.

The Forgotten Village (screenplay). 1941.

Sea of Cortez (with Edward F. Ricketts). 1941.

Bombs Away: The Story of a Bomber Team. 1942.

The Moon Is Down: A Play in Two Parts. 1942.

The Moon Is Down. 1943.

How Edith McGillcuddy Met R L S. 1943.

Lifeboat (screenplay). 1944.

Cannery Row. 1945.

A Medal for Benny (screenplay). 1945.

The Pearl (screenplay). 1945.

The Steinbeck Pocket Book. Ed. Pascal Covici. 1946.

The Pearl. 1947.

Vanderbilt Clinic. 1947.

The Wayward Bus. 1947.

The First Watch. 1947.

A Russian Journal (with Robert Capa). 1948.

The Red Pony (screenplay). 1949.

The Steinbeck Omnibus. 1950.

Burning Bright: A Play in Story Form. 1950.

Burning Bright (drama). 1951.

East of Eden. 1952.

Viva Zapata! (screenplay). 1952.

Short Novels. 1953.

Sweet Thursday. 1954.

Positano. 1954.

The Short Reign of Pippin IV: A Fabrication. 1957.

The Chrysanthemums. 1957.

Once There Was a War. 1958.

The Winter of Our Discontent. 1961.

Travels with Charley in Search of America. 1962.

Speech Accepting the Nobel Prize for Literature. 1962.

A Letter from John Steinbeck. 1964.

Letters to Alicia. 1965.

America and Americans. 1966.

The Journal of a Novel: The East of Eden *Letters.* 1969.

John Steinbeck: His Language. 1970.

Steinbeck: A Life in Letters. Ed. Elaine Steinbeck and Robert Wallsten. 1975.

The Acts of King Arthur and His Noble Knights, from the Winchester Manuscripts of Malory and Other Sources. 1976.

The Collected Poems of Amnesia Glasscock. 1976.

Letters to Elizabeth: A Selection of Letters from John Steinbeck to Elizabeth Otis. Ed. Florian J. Shasky and Susan F. Riggs. 1978.

Flight. 1979.

A Letter of Inspiration. 1980.

Selected Essays. Ed. Kiyoshi Nakayama and Hidekazu Hirose. 1981.

Your Only Weapon Is Your Work: A Letter by John Steinbeck to Dennis Murphy. 1985.

Uncollected Stories. Ed. Kiyoshi Nakayama. 1986.

Always Something to Do in Salinas. 1986.

Works about John Steinbeck

Anderson, Hilton. "Steinbeck's 'Flight.'" *Explicator* 28 (1969): Item 12.

Antico, John. "A Reading of Steinbeck's 'Flight.'" *Modern Fiction Studies* 11 (1965): 45–53.

Astro, Richard, and Hayashi, Tetsumaro, eds. *Steinback: The Man and His Work.* Corvalis: Oregon State University Press, 1971.

Astro, Richard. "Something That Happened: A Non-Teleological Approach to 'The Leader of the People.'" *Steinbeck Quarterly* VI (1973): 19–23.

Benson, Jackson D. *The True Adventures of John Steinbeck, Writer.* New York: Viking Press, 1984.

Benton, Robert M. "Realism, Growth, and Contrast in 'The Gift.'" *Steinbeck Quarterly* VI (1973): 3–9.

Busch, Christopher S. "Longing for the Lost Frontier: Steinbeck's Vision of Cultural Decline in 'The White Quail' and 'The Chrysanthemums.'" *Steinbeck Quarterly* 26 (1993): 81–90.

Davis, Robert Murray. *Steinbeck: A Colleciton of Critical Essays.* Englewood Cliffs, N.J.: Prentice Hall, 1972.

Ditsky, John M. "Steinbeck's 'Flight': The Ambiguity of Manhood." In Hayashi and Garcia, *A Study Guide to Steinbeck's* The Long Valley. Ann Arbor: Pierian, 1976.

Fontenrose, Joseph. *John Steinbeck: An Introduction and Interpretation.* New York: Holt, Rinehart and Winston, 1963.

Fontenrose, Joseph. "'The Harness.'" In Hayashi and Garcia, *A Study Guide to Steinbeck's* The Long Valley. Ann Arbor: Pierian, 1976.

French, Warren. *John Steinbeck.* New York: Twayne Publishers, 1961.

———. "'Johnny Bear': Steinbeck's 'Yellow Peril' Story." In Hayashi and Garcia, *A Study Guide to Steinbeck's* The Long Valley. Ann Arbor: Pierian, 1976.

Garcia, Reloy. "Steinbeck's 'The Snake': An Explication." In Hayashi and Garcia, *A Study Guide to Steinbeck's* The Long Valley. Ann Arbor: Pierian, 1976.

Girard, Maureen. "Steinbeck's 'Frightful' Story: The Conception and Evolution of 'The Snake.'" *San Jose Studies* 8 (1982): 33–40.

Gladstein, Mimi Reisel. *The Indestructible Woman in Faulkner, Hemingway, and Steinbeck.* Ann Arbor, MI: UMI Research Press, 1986.

Goldsmith, Arnold L. "Thematic Rhythm in 'The Red Pony.'" *College English* 26 (1965): 391–94.

Hadella, Charlotte. "Steinbeck's Cloistered Women." In *The Steinbeck Question: New Essays in Criticism.* Troy, NY: Whitston, 1993.

Hayashi, Tetsumaro, and Garcia, Reloy. *A Study Guide to Steinbeck's* The Long Valley. Ann Arbor: Pierian, 1976.

Hayashi, Tetsumaro, ed. *Steinbeck's Women: Essays in Criticism.* Muncie, IN: John Steinbeck Society of America, 1979.

Higdon, David Leon. "Dionysian Madness in Steinbeck's 'The Chrysanthemums'." *Classical and Modern Literature* 11 (1990): 59–65.

Hughes, R. S. *Beyond the Red Pony: A Reader's Companion to Steinbeck's Complete Short Stories.* Metuchen, NJ: The Scarecrow Press, 1987.

———. *John Steinbeck: A Study of the Short Fiction.* Boston: Twayne Publishers, 1989.

Johnson, Claudia Durst. *Understanding* Of Mice and Men, The Red Pony, *and* The Pearl. *A Student Casebook to Issues, Sources, and Historical Documents.* Westport, CT: Greenwood Press, 1997.

Johnston, Kenneth G. "Teaching the Short Story: An Approach to Steinbeck's 'Flight'." *Kansas English* 58 (1973): 4–11.

Kretschmer, Eugene P. "John Steinbeck's 'Flight' and Frank Waters' Flight from Fiesta: A Comparative Approach." In Adams, Charles L. (ed.). *Studies in Frank Waters, X: Connections.* Las Vegas: Frank Waters Soc., 1988.

Levant, Howard. "John Steinbeck's 'The Red Pony': A Study in Narrative Technique." *The Journal of Narrative Technique* 2 (1971): 77–85.

Lisca, Peter. *John Steinbeck: Nature and Myth.* New York: Crowell, 1978.

———. *The Wide World of John Steinbeck.* New Brunswick, NJ: Rutgers University Press, 1958.

Marcus, Mordecai. "The Lost Dream of Sex and Childbirth in 'The Chrysanthemums'." *Modern Fiction Studies* 11 (1965): 54–58.

Martin, Bruce K. "'The Leader of the People' Reexamined." *Studies in Short Fiction* VIII (1971): 423–32.

May, Charles E. "Myth and Mystery in Steinbeck's 'The Snake': A Jungian View." *Criticism* 15 (1973): 322–35.

McCarthy, Paul. *John Steinbeck.* New York: Frederick Ungar Publishing, 1980.

McElrath, Joseph R., Jr., Crisler, Jesse S., and Shillinglaw, Susan, eds. *John Steinbeck: The Contemporary Reviews.* Cambridge: Cambridge University Press, 1996.

McMahan, Elizabeth E. "'The Chrysanthemums': Study of a Woman's Sexuality." *Modern Fiction Studies* XIV (1968–9): 453–58.

Meyer, Michael J. "Fallen Adam: Another Look at Steinbeck's 'The Snake.'" In Noble, Donald R. (ed.), *The Steinbeck Question: New Essays in Criticism.* Troy, NY: Whitston, 1993.

Miller, William V. "Sexual and Spiritual Ambiguity in 'The Chrysanthemums.'" In Hayashi and Garcia, *A Study Guide to Steinbeck's* The Long Valley. Ann Arbor: Pierian, 1976.

Mitchell, Marilyn L. "'Steinbeck's Strong Women': Feminine Identity in the Short Stories." *Southwest Review* 61 (1976): 304–15.

Modern Fiction Studies, Special Issue: John Steinbeck XI (1965):1–104.

Morsberger, Robert E. "The Price of 'The Harness.'" *Steinbeck Quarterly* VI (1973): 24–26.

Noble, Donald R., ed. *The Steinbeck Question: New Essays in Criticism.* Troy, NY: Whitston, 1993.

Osborne, William R. "The Texts of Steinbeck's 'The Chrysanthemums'." *Modern Fiction Studies* XII (1966–67): 479–84.

Owens, Louis. *John Steinbeck's Revision of America.* Athens, GA: University of Georgia Press, 1985.

Parini, Jay. *John Steinbeck: A Biography.* London: Heinemann, 1994.

Pearce, Howard D. "Steinbeck's 'The Leader of the People': Dialectic and Symbol." *Papers on Language and Literature* VIII (1972): 415–26.

Pellow, C. Kenneth. "'The Chrysanthemums' Revisited." *Steinbeck Quarterly* 22 (1989): 8–16.

Peterson, Richard F. "The Grail Legend and Steinbeck's 'The Great Mountains.'" *Steinbeck Quarterly* VI (1973): 9–15.

Piacentino, Edward J. "Patterns of Animal Imagery in Steinbeck's 'Flight.'" *Studies in Short Fiction* 17 (1980): 437–43.

Piwinski, David J. "Floral Gold in Steinbeck's 'The Chrysanthemums.'" *Notes on Contemporary Literature* 27 (1997): 4–5.

Railsback, Brian. "A Frog, a Bear, a Snake, and the Human Species: Uncomfortable Reflections in John Steinbeck's Grotesques." In Meyer, Michael J. (ed.), *Literature and the Grotesque.* Amsterdam: Rodopi, 1995.

Renner, Stanley. "Sexual Idealism and Violence in 'The White Quail.'" *Steinbeck Quarterly* 17 (1984): 76–87.

———. "Mary Teller and Sue Bridehead: Birds of a Feather in 'The White Quail' and Jude the Obscure." *Steinbeck Quarterly* 18 (1985): 35–45.

———. "The Real Woman Inside the Fence in 'The Chrysanthemums.'" *Modern Fiction Studies* 31 (1985): 305–17.

Satyanarayana, M. R. "'And Then the Child Becomes a Man': Three Initiation Stories of John Steinbeck." *Indian Journal of American Studies* 1(1971): 87–93.

Shuman, R. Baird. "Initiation Rites in Steinbeck's *The Red Pony.*" *English Journal* 59 (1970): 1252–55.

Simmonds, Roy S. "The Original Manuscripts of Steinbeck's 'The Chrysanthemums.'" *Steinbeck Quarterly* VII (1974): 102–11.

———. "The First Publication of Steinbeck's 'The Leader of the People.'" *Steinbeck Quarterly* VIII (1975): 13–18.

Simpson, Arthur L., Jr. "'The White Quail': A Portrait of an Artist." In Hayashi and Garcia, *A Study Guide to Steinbeck's* The Long Valley. Ann Arbor: Pierian, 1976.

Steinbeck, Elaine, and Wallsten, Robert. *Steinbeck: A Life in Letters.* New York: Viking Press, 1975.

Sullivan, Ernest W., II. "The Cur in 'The Chrysanthemums.'" *Studies in Short Fiction* 16 (1979): 215–17.

Sweet, Charles A., Jr. "Ms. Elisa Allen and Steinbeck's 'The Chrysanthemums.'" *Modern Fiction Studies* 20 (1974): 210–14.

Timmerman, John H. *John Steinbeck's Fiction: The Aesthetics of the Road Taken.* Norman: University of Oklahoma Press, 1986.

———. *The Dramatic Landscape of Steinbeck's Short Stories.* University of Oklahoma Press, 1990.

Tiwari, I. D. *Steinbeck's Heroes in his Short Stories and Novels.* South Gamri, Delhi: Rekha Publishing House, 1992.

Vogel, Dan. "Steinbeck's 'Flight': The Myth of Manhood." *College English* 23 (1961): 225–26.

West, Philip J. "Steinbeck's 'The Leader of the People': A Crisis in Style." *Western American Literature* V (1970): 137–40.

Weston, Cheryl, and Knapp, John V. "Profiles of the Scientific Personality: John Steinbeck's 'Snake.'" *Mosaic* 22 (1989): 87–99.

Woodward, Robert H. "Steinbeck's 'The Promise.'" *Steinbeck Quarterly* VI (1973): 15–19.

Work, James C. "Coordinate Forces in 'The Leader of the People.'" *Western American Literature* XVI (1982): 279–89.

Index of
Themes and Ideas

STEINBECK, JOHN: biography of, 11–15, 70–71; Lawrence and, 9